From
To. Jefferson
Thanks for your
support

Shot twice in the head but far from dead:

The story of a juvenile delinquent

A True Story by Maurice Young

11-10-22

BK PUBLISHING CO.

A Message to my Family,

I would like to apologize first and foremost for all the hell I've put you all through. I allowed drugs and ignorance to take control over my life but now that I've come face to face with death and walked away from it I can honestly say that I've learned my lesson and became a better person overall. I will never again put you all through what I put you through during those dark years of my life. Most of all thank you for forgiving me and allowing me back into this household. I love all of you with all my heart and with every ounce of blood inside my body. I thank you very much.

A message to you,

If the person reading this is the person who shot me, I want to tell you that I thank you for slowing me down and I really thank you for waking my stubborn ass up. Most of all I thank you for doing what you did because you gave my son the father he deserves not that drug addict that I was. You know who you are. I thank you.

Love,

M.Y

CHAPTERS

Introduction

ly name is Maurice Young and this is my autobiography. In iis novel I will take you along the journey of my life. My main bjective while taking you down this long dark path is to open ie eyes of misguided youth today and have them learn from iy previous mistakes in an attempt to keep them far away om the road that I was once along. Also, it is my hope that iey can observe the consequences which stemmed from the fe I once lived and will decide to choose the complete pposite; living the rest of their lives as positive and roductive citizens. This book will also provide some useful ps for avoiding trouble altogether.

Chapter 1

The Beginning

Most people speculate that I got all my corrupt behavior from my father but I'm going to take responsibility for what I became; a deceptive and devious juvenile delinquent. This is the story of me, Maurice Young, as a juvenile delinquent that was also conniving, disobedient, and disrespectful towards my mother and hurt her constantly by my negative actions. I'll tell you the truth about where and when the devious actions and delinquency began. It all started at the age of five. Growing up I lived in two completely different worlds. During the week I lived in my mother's world which primarily consisted of lectures on the difference between right and wrong, manners, proper etiquette and what it meant to be respectful to adults. We also did a lot of preparatory educational activities so that I'd be advanced when it was time for me to enroll into school. During the weekend I lived in my grandmother's and father's world which had no real structure. I was my grandmother's only grandchild on my father's side therefore she allowed most of my corrupt behavior to occur without punishment which ranged from me stealing her 14ct gold diamond ring to walking out of corner stores and supermarkets with merchandise I didn't purchase. I was my father's first-born so he used that as an excuse for the lack of parenting he displayed. My first few school years in Catholic school I was considered a terror and a habitual liar. By the second grade I was behaving so poorly my teacher started to write bad behavior notes inside my workbook.

In fear of getting disciplined, I came up with a clever and deceptive plan that would keep me out of trouble with the bad behavior notes. At that time, I knew how to trace comic book characters identically and I also had perfect penmanship, so I began to trace over my mother's signature so persistently that in less than three days I was able to sign her name identical to her signature. As luck would have it, the notes were so horrific, but they were still getting signed without any response or concern, so my teacher demanded a parent teacher conference to expose who was the real culprit behind the signatures. It took them only a matter of seconds to come to the conclusion that I was forging my mother's signature. After I was disciplined for doing that, my misbehavior did not stop; instead I started stealing anything and everything that wasn't nailed to the floor. I became a kleptomaniac to the very definition of the word. It started out with five cent candies at the corner stores and supermarkets then I graduated to electronic devices from my classmates and teachers. My mother foresaw what type of trouble was brewing for her while raising me even though some of her peers would try to tell her it was only a phase, she wasn't convinced and believed my actions were deliberate.

In an effort to slow me down and guide me in the right direction, she introduced me to the truth, and I started studying to become a Jehovah Witness. Introducing me to religion calmed me down a lot and I stopped stealing and lying for almost two years but as the years passed by, I deserted my religion and went back to my old ways of stealing and lying. When the devious actions dug deeper into my mother's heart, I argued with her that it wasn't my intentions to hurt her however my actions proved otherwise. My first childhood obbery was towards my father at the age of seven. He had everal 32 gallon empty water containers filled with silver ollars and fifty cent pieces. Everyday I would ask my dad for noney and after many failed attempts I felt as though he left ne with no other choice, so I began filling my pockets with the oined dollars and fifty cent pieces. Desperate for ompanionship, I started handing out the fifty cent pieces and ilver dollars to all my childhood friends in the neighborhood. fter I gave away all the coined dollars I had stolen, I became ery greedy and went back for more. Only this time, all the oined dollars were gone so I ransacked my father's room. Vhile ransacking his room, I came across a burgundy satchel lled with paper bills and among the bills was a rare Indian lue headed five-dollar bill that dated back to 1935. As a naive hild I thought the bill was a counterfeit, so I decided to try and pend the bill even though I thought it wasn't really worth nything.

ater on that day, I walked into the neighborhood corner store nd picked out a few items to buy with the bill. I wanted to eceive the Korean clerk so badly but not only did I not deceive the clerk, the clerk was able to get over on me instead. After I got home and my father discovered where I spent the bill, he gripped me up and dragged me back to the store where I spent the rare currency and tried to make the Korean clerk let him search through the register for the bill. The clerk refused. He even offered the clerk a fifty-dollar bill and requested a trade but the clerk must have done his homework on the bill and knew it's worth so he declined the trade. That's when I discovered how I foolishly spent a rare type of currency that was worth way more than fifty bucks. When my father told me how rare that bill was valuing over forty five thousand dollars, I didn't believe him at first because he never talked with me and showed me its value. He pulled out a collector's item's hand guide and then one of his friends told me how much the bill was worth and I was shocked. I still had my doubts but that's when I realized that I did in fact purchase a snickers candy bar and some mamba gummy candy with a rare currency worth over forty-five thousand dollars.

My father then told me that I better get real good at sports because that rare bill was supposed to be used for my college ition. My stealing didn't end there. Once again, desperately seeking friendship and acceptance, I stole a 14ct gold diamond ring out of my grandmother's jewelry box and gave it to my friend. When my grandmother discovered this, not only did this hurt her but it also hurt my mother because she purchased the 14ct gold diamond ring for my grandmother for her birthday one year. After the diamond ring was retrieved, it still did not stop my deceit and thievery. After ransacking through my grandmother's dressers, I came across many signed valid checks. I stole those as well and traded them for baseball cards. After the checks were retrieved, instead of punishing me, my grandmother started taking me hiking at valley green and I stopped stealing for a little while. We also traveled up and down the whole east coast and some states down south.

Unfortunately, after I stopped stealing for a very short period of time, I started playing with matches and lighters. I became a firebug which started out with me smoking the marijuana roaches remaining in the ashtray left by my father. I guess he figured that me being so young, I didn't pick up on what he did but I was far from the truth. I noticed that he smoked weed and was well aware of everything. I was so deceptive that after I caught my first little buzz, I began tricking my father more and more in order to get a hit. After he rolled up a fresh marijuana cigar and took a few puffs of it, I'd lie and say, "Dad, grandma wants you upstairs" and he would put the marijuana cigar out, lay it down, and would go to see what my grandma wanted. Within a good five minute window, I would relight and puff on the marijuana cigar. I remember one time I smoked enough of it to become fully high. Man was I hungry and confused! Everything looked awkward and the experience was an eye opener to me because I never felt that bad ever in my life and I promised myself that I would never smoke anything ever again.

While still hungry and craving a snack, I walked to the basement to grab something to eat. After looking in the freezer and all through the cabinets, I noticed a Ziploc bag of what I thought were salted pretzel Rods. I grabbed a handful and stuffed my face with the so-called pretzels. After I digested a bunch of them, my dad rushed downstairs to see what I was doing. Things were way too quiet which normally meant that I was up to no good. He ran to see what mess I was getting into and he found me in the basement and realized exactly what it was. He grabbed and shook the hell out of me then yelled WHAT THE HELL ARE YOU DOING!" I responded, "Eating pretzels." He snatched the Ziploc bag out of my hands and said, "Do these look like fucking pretzels to you?" Spitting out the remains, I realized I was eating huge buds of marijuana.

Afterwards I had a severe stomachache and my head was throbbing, but he still made me stand in the corner for a few hours anyway. When my time in the corner was over, I went upstairs to my grandmother's room and angrily started lighting plastic roses and pieces of paper on fire. I was highly aggravated during this time in my life so I would light things on fire to work out my frustration. The flames were so amazing to me but they grew out of control and the flaming pieces of plastic started falling onto the carpet. My dad smelled the smoke and ran upstairs to stomp out the flames. Then he hit my hand real hard with a broom stick handle which felt like my hand had broken. At that point my pyromaniac stages were quickly rectified but I still had to scrub the burnt portions of the carpet clean as punishment. Instead of him just dealing with me himself when situations like these would occur, he would call my mother and complain then send me home packing which further placed the burden on my mom and made me feel unwanted. This would stress her out to the point the edges of her hair started to turn grey. I knew it was from the grief I was causing her but in my grandmother's eyes I could do no wrong. When I did bad things, she rarely disciplined me. The catholic school I was attending at the time was fed up with my behavior problems so they gave my mother an ultimatum; to either remove me from their school before the next semester or take a chance that I would start to behave but if I didn't I would be expelled and all tuition would be forfeited. This was when it was decided that I would attend public school.

In 1999, I enrolled in the second largest public school located in the northwest region. This was also the same year That I lost my grandma. I believe that this is when things went from bad to worse. While in public school I was constantly teased about my weight problem so I would get into at least three fights a

reek. Each time I was suspended my mom would have to eave
ork so she could talk to the dean about my behavior issues
nd how poorly I got along with my classmates. However, this
idn't hurt my mother as bad as when I was stealing from my
amily because I was defending myself. As the years went on
nd I began to go through puberty, I got bigger in weight and
as picked on even more than usual. Around this time I was
atching a lot of gang related movies and one night I watched
 documentary about these gang bangers from New Jersey that
ere into sex, money, and murder. Bloods everywhere feared
nem and respected their set because they were ruthless, and
ney went around slicing their enemies faces open with razor
lades. It was at that very moment that I knew I wanted to
ecome a gang banger because they were feared and
espected and I was sick of getting picked on. So I purchased a
lack bandana and hung it out of my back right pocket. My
lassmates would say *you're supposed to hang it out your left*
ocket, but I ignored their advice because in my mind I knew
hat I was doing. I would even tie the bandana over my face.
his often disturbed my teachers so they would call my

mother while she was working which interrupted her business.

My plan was to put fear into the hearts of the students who teased me but it didn't work on all but one classmate. At first he wasn't intimidated by me wearing the bandana because I was all bark and no bite. He would tease me by calling me fat and making elephant noises behind me as I walked up the stairs. After I beat him up a few times, he took a break from teasing me however this only lasted a short period because he started back up with the insults.

One day I asked my dad to buy me some Air Jordans. He said he wasn't spending over a hundred dollars for sneakers and he purchased me a used lawn mower and weed whacker to instill some type of drive and legit hustle in me. He wanted me to start buying my own stuff and stop being spoiled rotten. I started my own business and made twenty dollars per lawn. I made my friend Scarface a fifty percent split partner because we used his dad's office equipment to make flyers to circulate our names throughout the neighborhood. After I saved two undred dollars I started looking on-line for BB guns. My earch ended when I found two realistic looking BB guns on ie Walmart website but I didn't have a card to purchase nline so I talked my friend called Whiteboy into going with ie to buy one in person because I was again desperate for ompanionship. I told Whiteboy I'd pay half of how much his wn would cost so we caught the bus to Plymouth meeting iall to go to a Dicks Sporting Goods store because there iasn't a Walmart near our neighborhood and we figured ihatever Walmart had Dicks had to have also. We then walked bout two miles down Chemical road to Dicks. When we rrived we were told that because the location of the store was ɔ close to the White Marsh Philadelphia county line they ieren't allowed to sell pellet guns but the clerk looked out and ɔld us about the Walmart near gulph mills road. He confirmed iat they would sell us the BB guns with no problem so we ialked back to the bus depot only to find out the Walmart we iere seeking was 4 miles up Germantown Pike. We decided to ike it but when we finally arrived at the counter there was a ig sign with red letters that read **in order to purchase any**

type of pellet gun a Pennsylvania I.D showing proof of age 18 or older was required so I looked around and I noticed a middle aged black man near us. I used my slick talk and deceived him into thinking the BB guns were a birthday gift for our uncle. The man was gullible and he agreed to take our money and buy them for us. Our hearts filled with joy and excitement and we returned home and started shooting at everything except cars and houses. Some of our targets were stop signs and trash cans and even each other. One day he shot me in my left hand with the BB gun and the pellet went through my skin. It got stuck inside my hand and I became afraid thinking I was going to get lead poisoning, so I dug the pellet out of my hand with a kitchen knife. Afterwards I noticed my brother's SUV creeping slowly down the block and he caught us shooting trash cans and stop signs. As soon as I saw his car approaching, I quickly passed off my BB gun to Whiteboy and he held on to it but he was later arrested for taking it to school. Fortunately for me when my brother caught me doing something that I had no business doing he never tried to discipline me by hitting me but he always took the military approach so when we got home he made me do one hundred and fifty pushups and sit ups.

At the time I was still obsessed with gang life and a complete loser, so my mother told my older brother what I was going through on a daily basis at school for some mentorship. He decided it was time for him to train me so he took me in for the whole summer of sixth grade. He had this method called to condition knuckles. What he used was a big bucket of sand tied to a wooden broom handle and he made me curl it many times. This practice helped develop my biceps then he showed me the method that conditioned my knuckles to become rock solid. He also had me grind my fist in the sand. That summer I did hundreds of sit-ups and probably thousands of push-ups. He also taught me the basics of the martial art WUSHU and had me training with grown men. When the summer ended, I grew from a 5"5 short pudgy loser to a 5"9 tall dark and handsome athletic built young man. Before I left him that summer, I had the worst dream I could possibly have. In the dream I was sitting on my front steps talking on the phone then a man in his mid-twenties parked his white 7 series BMW across the street from my house, got out and walked towards me nonchalantly. He pulled out a gun and shot me in my head. I didn't die immediately but I fell down to the sidewalk and crawled to the corner of my block. The dream made me really nervous and never again did I sit on my front steps to do anything. When I returned back to school my arms which once jiggled like gelatin were now rock-hard biceps and that sloppy gut of a stomach I had was transformed into a chiseled six-pack. I went from a fat unattractive dude to a confident female charmer stud and my life started to change.

Chapter 2

Ego tripping

fter I was transformed into that athletic proper fit young
1an, I was top three on the popularity scale at my school. The
easing stopped and I went on an ego trip. As far as my fighting
kills went I knew for a fact I could go blow for blow with
nyone but I felt defenseless against someone that would be
rmed so I went around my neighborhood looking to purchase
 handgun.

nly one person came through for me, the mole. He sold me a
80 caliber Smith and Wesson pistol for eighty dollars and his
lder brother got me my first job at Burger King. While
vorking there all the bosses were old Indian Hindu men who
10ught that we were all young dumb ignorant black kids. But
ve constantly had schemes going on; like while working the
rive-thru window we wouldn't ring up the orders. Instead we
vould pocket the money and do the math in our heads to
eturn the customers their correct change. One day the general
1anager manually punched in his I.D number code into my

register. This turned out to be a big mistake because I memorized the digits and started simulating money from the register. When you simulate money, the computer says the amount that was simulated. After already counting money in the register, me and Scarface simulated eighty dollars out of each register after every shift. One day I got into an altercation with the guy who got me the job. We both got fired, but after I was fired I became highly motivated so I quickly got another job at Rita's water ice.

One day I decided I wanted a real gun so I began asking around and found someone who would sell me a pistol. The person that sold me the .380 pistol said he got it from a classmate, but I later found out that it belonged to his mother.

After purchasing the pistol, me and White boy stuck up a few teenagers from Chestnut hill in the summer of 2005. This is when I really started showing my ass off. Everything my brother taught me about leadership and individuality I disregarded and instead I turned into a follower and started going along with my squad. We would smoke weed every day nd beat up grown men for their wallets and personal items. I nly had one rule; no women and no senior citizens. I would)llow my niggas from Stenton Ave to across the city. We went verywhere and traveled in packs of no less than five people. ⸱ we noticed someone with a briefcase or expensive jewelry n, then we robbed them of all their valuables.

aturday September 11th 2005 was my brother's birthday. I ought him a double CD package that the rapper Nelly had eleased that year. Me and my squad from Stenton avenue ʒere behind an apartment complex getting high before we left ɔr a party that we were invited to smoking. During this eriod, smoking weed wasn't just a high to me it was a festyle. I needed weed in order to be who I was at the time nd it gave me the confidence I needed to talk to any woman I esired. I felt superior to everyone around me and no one ould tell me otherwise. After we finished smoking, we ecided to leave for the party, but my phone rang. It was the irthday man and he wanted me to meet up with him. I nmediately became paranoid and nervous. So I lied about ʒhere I was in order to buy myself some time so I could air out. My brother grew impatient because I was taking too long to meet him where I said I would so he called me back three times in a row. I sprayed some AXE body fragrance on me to mask the smell and then I walked over to where he was waiting for me. My friends offered to hold my pistol until I finished with my brother but because I had major trust issues, I refused the offer. After I approached my brother's vehicle, I made up tons of excuses about why I couldn't get in the SUV. He became suspicious but was the type that didn't want a speck of dust in his car, so I used his obsession with cleanliness to my advantage. I said, "Bro I'll give you what I got you later I sat in mud so I can't get in the car." He said, "Alright I'll grab my gift later" and drove off.

I congratulated myself for convincing him to allow me to meet up with him later because he had a nose for trouble. It was like he could smell when something wasn't right. Then I went home to get fresh for the party and on the way there I hoped my mom was either at work or asleep. It turns out she wasn't at work nor was she asleep. When I arrived, I went straight to my room to hide the pistol and change for the party.

had the pistol concealed in the area between your testicles
nd rectum in my pants. As I heard her footsteps approaching
1y door, I stripped damn near naked and tried to hide the
istol, but I wasn't quick enough. Due to all the weight I had
)st over the summer that my brother trained me, I had gained
: right back eating free food at Burger King so when she
pened the door, the gun fell to the floor. My mother became
ery enraged and she started beating my ass to the point I
idn't want anything to do with guns anymore. As she
1hooped me, she started throwing these insanely quick and
nbelievable hard jabs. The first combination caught me
ompletely off guard. My face looked like I was stung by a
warm of wasps. My reflexes kicked in after being highly
·ained to block attacks, so I started blocking her punches. The
1ay that I was taught to block was to cuff your hand over the
ttacker's arm and throw the punch away from you. My mom
onsidered that as me striking her back I tried to explain that
's an unintentional reflex and that I couldn't help it. I wanted
) lead her to believe I was done with being bad. However,
othing was going to make me change. I loved everything that

I was doing deep down inside. My lifestyle of smoking weed, drinking, and fucking a different broad every day was exciting. What fourteen year old in their right mind would give up those things over a five minute ass whooping?

She packed up all of my clothes and called my father to come get me and take me to his home in Delaware. My mother informed him that I was going to live with him because she was fed up with my behavioral problems. After living in Delaware for two weeks my mom called him and after speaking to her my father said to me, "What, ya mom don't trust me to tend to your needs?" I said " I'm really not sure." Then he asked me if I was calling her and complaining about the living arrangements? I said "No, why?" He replied, "Because she keeps blowing up my phone asking about you." I had my doubts but like I said, whenever he didn't feel like dealing with me he'd send me back to my mom's. Then he told me "Sunday night I'm going to humble your spoiled ass by grabbing you some corny uniform pants. It looks like you got all name brand shit. I never had no name brand clothes nigga that's why you acting up because whatever you want they just ive it to you." In my mind I thought *that is a lie* because I tayed with a job.

ne day I saw his jeans on the floor and me being the thief that had turned into, I ran in his pockets and pulled out what ppeared to be three thousand dollars. I wanted half but I new that would've been too obvious so I only took eighty ollars. I refused to be seen wearing those straight legged ickies they would've cramped my style. Thankfully my 1other was the one who caught me with the pistol and not the olice so my father dropped me off back home with my mother fter some time. I swore up and down that I'd never even think bout obtaining another firearm and she forgave me and viped the slate clean then. Everything went back to normal nd I went right back at it, hanging with the squad, blowing ees, and having sex with random girls. My criminal record vas still clean at the time but that didn't last long.

got invited to see my cousin off on his prom and I noticed the id from my class that used to tease me constantly was there 1 the crowd. He got in the photograph with all the cousins and confused, I walked over and asked my older cousins what was going on. They began to explain how me and him were related the whole time and suggested we put all petty differences aside. My oldest cousin pulled me to the side and said, "Since you're built like a grown man, act like one." He asked me to watch our cousin's back saying "You know he's going to need you with all the trash he talks." After he said that. I felt obligated to look after him and let the past go. Yes, the same student that tormented my whole public school experience I decided to forgive. One day a new kid transferred to our class from another school and him and my cousin started displaying ignorance towards each other. They were determined to keep their feud going but they battled it out by freestyle rapping against each other. They were both trash when it came to rapping but I'm glad that situation ended positively.

Chapter 3

The first scratch on my criminal record

very Monday during gym class we were allowed to do whatever activities we wanted to do. My cousin, the new kid, and myself started up a game of rough house. I had a feeling this was a bad idea because, if you're not familiar with the game, whoever scores was able to shoot foul shots. The first person to make a foul shot calls the rules for the game. After I made the first foul shot I decided to make the rules all regulation call shots until you died. When it came to foul shots that meant you kept shooting your foul shots until you missed and block shots would take you back to zero points. I also made the rule that the game goes to forty five and because I was the tallest no one could actually block my shot. By the age of fourteen I was smoking weed heavy but I still scored twenty six points. My cousin had thirty-five points but he was uncoordinated. My cousin blocked the new kid's shot and the new kid had zero and became furious. He was determined to make a comeback and was able to score 15 points. I had many chances to block his shot and take him back to zero points but I choose not to be so competitive. I was one hundred percent sure that I was going to win that session of rough house so during the rest of the game basically the two of them played one on one nonchalantly while I just stood there collecting rebounds and laying up the ball for easy points. The new kid was real close to a victory but then out of nowhere my cousin runs up on the side of the new kid and blocks his shot from the side taking him back to zero. For the second time the new kid calls foul and my cousin tells him, "Man up because there's no fouls in rough house dick head." After he said that, the new kid felt provoked and embarrassed so he threw the ball at my cousin's head followed by a flurry of jabs to his mouth. The school officer gripped up the new kid and placed him in the in-house suspension room. My cousin attempted to rush after the new kid to retaliate but I gripped him up and quietly informed him that I would handle the situation later. I also reminded him of the talk the dean had with us which implied that the next time either of us was suspended we would be expelled.

should've kept that in mind before I retaliated back. My cousin calmed down and after the next class we went to lunch. The in-house suspension room was wide open so I looked around checking out my surroundings. That's when I noticed the new kids girlfriend, who ironically happened to be my ex, sitting where he could see her. I wanted to mess with his head so I walked over to her and caressed her lower back. The sensation got me aroused so I sat directly behind her with my legs open and my penis on her butt, then I started rubbing her lower back. She giggled then asked me why I was doing this in front of her boyfriend. I replied, "Because he's a cold cornball." When lunch ended I was plotting on how I was going to retaliate and get revenge for my cousin. The new kid is released from the room and he takes the front stairs to the third floor, so I took the back stairs. We arrived on the third floor at the same time and I saw him leaning on the lockers holding his crotch looking at me as if he were invincible. I approached him with my left hand open anticipating to strike him but first I asked him, "Why did you do that sucker shit to my cousin?" He replied "Look man, fuck you and your cousin so get out of my face with the bullshit." I displayed a devilish grin and then swiftly threw one jab to his jawbone. He held his mouth, moaned, jumped up and down, and after I saw blood leak from his mouth I nonchalantly walked to the bathroom to hideout. I let ten minutes pass by thinking the situation had died down. I went back to my class and everyone was hype bringing unneeded attention to me. I told everyone to be cool because I was trying to keep a low profile and sneak out of school before they find out what I did. The very second I said that, the school officer called me out of the class and then asked me why I hit him. I denied ever putting my hands on him and after getting questioned for over ten minutes, I made up a story that he was pissed because I was putting the moves on his girl so he approached me and pushed me and I hit him in self-defense.

The officer told me that I was lucky that I went to school in Chestnut hill because if I went to a middle school like Leeds the police would have arrested me for aggravated assault right on the spot. I was suspended and expelled two weeks before graduation. After that incident I felt like the biggest idiot and ly mother was called to come remove me off of the school's roperty. Three days later I received a subpoena in the mail nforming me that there was a warrant for my arrest for the ssault on the student. It instructed me to turn myself in nmediately so my mother called my aunt to see if we could et a ride to the 35th district in the morning. She agreed but efore I turned myself in I got a big breakfast. One of my ssociates had told me that I better eat real good before I turn nyself in because all jail food is disgusting and I didn't know rhen I was coming home. When we walked inside the precinct ly mother asked for the detective whose name was on the ubpoena. She informed us that I broke the student's jaw in no different places and then she placed me under arrest for ne aggravated assault. I sat in the juvenile holding cell for at :ast ten hours and as the day went by numerous males were laced under custody for many different reasons. I was ervous because this was my first arrest but they all told me) relax because this was my first offense and I would probably et off easy. I was hoping they were right. That night I was sent) the Youth Study Center (YSC). Although I was fourteen, I was big for my age 5"9 all muscle and none of the other juveniles believed I was only fourteen. A few days later I had an interview to determine whether I was eligible for release. The woman asked my mother how I acted at home and my mom covered for me telling her I was good. I never gave her feedback, was always on time for my curfew, so I was released on home detention without the ankle bracelet. I missed work that entire weekend, but my boss had a huge crush on my brother so after he explained what happened I was still able to keep my job. I was assigned a youth advocate worker as well. He was really cool with me because I was his only juvenile with a legit job. We went to cookouts and Phillies baseball games and then my preliminary hearing came up informing me what judge I was assigned to. The hearing was over in a matter of seconds all I had to say was not guilty and it was over. I was assigned to the Honorable Judge Lori Dumas.

The last name sounded familiar, but I couldn't figure out where I knew it from at first. My advocate told me she was cool but stern and that she could smell a bullshit story from a mile away. My stomach clenched up and then I became nervous

ecause my whole defense was a lie. On my first day of trial I
managed to persuade a classmate into being a witness for my
case. I instructed him to tell the judge I was provoked and was
forced to strike the plaintiff after he struck me first. After
walking into the courthouse I had to turn in my cell phone
ecause it had a camera on it and as I waited in line, the young
man's mother was waiting behind me. After I checked in my
cell, my mother and I went to the waiting area where I was
approached by a public defender. She suggested I take a deal
and plead guilty to a misdemeanor. My mother quickly
interjected and asked the Public Defender to explain clearly
what I was admitting to and as we waited I saw the boy I
assaulted walk over to him. I extended my hand for a
handshake and he greeted my hand. As we shook hands I said,
"Yo bull I'm sorry that whole episode was on some bullshit we
ood?" He said, "Yeah water under the bridge." So we walked
inside the Judge's Chambers. As the judge came out to address
the court, I had a surprised satisfying expression on my face
ecause the judge was my childhood friend's mother.
immediately she said, "Maurice is that you?" I replied, "Yes

your Honor" then I held my head down in shame. She addressed the court informing them that she knew me personally and that I must have been highly provoked to have broken the plaintiff's jaw with a single punch. I plead guilty to a misdemeanor then was assigned to 50 hours of anger management and because this was my first offense she put the crime on my record as a deferred adjudication which meant that if I stayed out of the court system for two years the charge would be removed from my record. However, I wasn't off the hook yet and I still had thirteen thousand six hundred and fifty-five dollars in restitution to pay. They knew there was no legit way for a fourteen year old boy to come up with that much money so I was put in a community service program and I was able to choose what rec center I wanted to work at. So I chose Finley recreation Center. They gave the money I earned directly to the courts which was six dollars an hour. I put in so much work to pay off the debt that after I completed my community service, I was informed that all I had to do was complete my anger management hours which didn't start until the third week of the upcoming school year and I would be off robation. I was stuck in the house basically the whole ummer until I brought up to my youth advocate the fact that was his most responsible juvenile and that he should bend ie rules for me and give me a curfew. He agreed but I took iat opportunity to start back smoking and hanging with my 'iends from the neighborhood which is also around the same me I started taking three to four Xanax pills at a time. I turned) popping pills because weed wasn't working for me anymore nd I remembered hearing that popping two Xanax had the ame effect as smoking three L's of marijuana. I would buy five ollars worth of marijuana at a time along with two to four anax just to get high.

he person I was buying my drugs from considered himself as ne of my old heads so he began to lecture me about how I was)olishly spending fifty dollars a week on nickel bags just to moke when I could buy quantity from him and sell my own icks. Business wise it seemed to be the smarter route so I ontinued buying weight from him until the quality of his roduct took a huge nosedive. Then I took my business to nother popular dealer in my neighborhood. He was known for his high potent product and I was making ok money with my last product but it wasn't enough to maintain the type of lifestyle I was living so I knew I had to upgrade to a more addictive narcotic. I was still fairly new to the game so I had no idea what I wanted to move onto until I was smoking with my supplier and he intentionally pulls out twenty five twenty dollar bills and counted them in front me. I counted in my head as he's doing the same. When he finished I had to ask him how he made five hundred dollars and he just looked at me and said, "This would be twice as much if my aunt would stop sneaking in my room and stealing my coke." At that very moment I knew what I was going to start selling coke as well.

Chapter 4

The Military Academy

wo months later, the issue of me being removed from the ublic-school system was mentioned again. My former rincipal wanted to send me to the alternative school CEP but 1e Honorable Judge Dumas didn't agree that I would be better ff at CEP so she called numerous principals and Deans trying) give me hope of attending a regular public school again. One entleman reached out because he had done such favors for l-behaved students before. The school was the Philadelphia Iilitary Academy.

Iy first day attending Philadelphia Military Academy, Mr. Vright, the principal, called me to his office for a private 1troduction. He immediately jumped straight down my throat /ithout hesitation and informed me that every student he ave the same chance he was giving me couldn't handle the ıles of the stern military academy and was kicked out of the cademy. He told me the same thing was going to happen with 1e. In fear of his prediction, I joined the school's physical fitness team. I only did it to occupy my time and stay out of trouble. One afternoon the team and I were jogging around on the Germantown's football team track chanting drills. After we did a mile I decided to walk the fatigue off and as I walked my muscles were shining, veins pulsating out of my forehead, and then the starting quarterback for the Germantown bears hollered at me asking "Yo bull how old are you?" I replied "Fourteen." He said "Damn youngbull you're my dad's size, we need you on the squad."

Afterwards he instructed me to follow him to meet the one and only coach Hawkins. He also introduced me to the defensive coordinator coach Goodwin. Coach Hawkins asked if I wanted to be the only freshmen on the varsity team no tryout required. I told him that I needed permission from my probation officer. He made me call my P.O on the spot and he agreed to allow me to play but I wasn't 100% on the team. I still needed a medical clearance. After I turned in the medical clearance I had a pick from five different numbers nine, fifty-eight, eighteen, sixty-nine and forty five. After hearing the numbers, I automatically turned on my knowledge about rearms, 69 being too sexual 9 being too weak, and when mall caliber pistols fire a round usually the bullet spirals and ; moving so fast it goes in and out the target on the other hand .45 caliber pistol when it's fired the bullets never spiral they umble doing a front flip motion severely damaging whatever : hits. That's what I wanted to be known as, the high caliber veapon that destroyed anything in its path and those were my trong points agility, speed, endurance, strength and my incredible high tolerance for pain. Coach was thrilled with my erformance and by my sixth football game I was starting as a 'efensive Tackle. I even started over a few seniors and they icknamed me 'anger management' because every Thursday had to leave practice early for my anger management ession.

he first game I played in was Germantown versus Dobbins nd it took no effort for me to complete tackles in that game. I ad two sacks and two forced fumbles and then I was switched) the kickoff team temporarily because of my speed, accuracy nd high tolerance for pain. I sprinted down the field towards ie ball handler and I broke through their kick return defense, grabbed the ball handler by his waist then slammed him down making him fumble. I knew I had found my new calling by playing football but I was lazy when I came to perfecting my skills. Meanwhile in school I was constantly getting in trouble for not shaving my facial hair to meet the military school requirements but my physical performance and grades were good enough for me to get promoted to cadet Sergeant and platoon leader. Since I was in charge of my entire class, I decided to use the opportunity to start stealing laptops, handheld game stations, and anything else that was worth money. After noticing that there were a lot of potential clients to sell my product to, I started selling drugs in school as well and I was trying to acquire as much money as I possibly could.

A bigger opportunity occurred when my S.A.T prep class started going to a computer lab in the school to work on our essay writing skills. We went into the lab twice every week and I called this room Candy Land because it had all the goods in it. During my first class in the Candy Land classroom, I noticed about twenty-five open white boxes on the floor. My premonition skills were on point so I tapped a classmate whom I knew wouldn't tell or run his mouth and told him to look out for me. He agreed and I knew whatever was in those boxes was worth major money so I unzipped my duffle bag and quickly snatched the item that was in the box and put it inside. My eyes opened wide open after seeing it was a state of the art HP Pavilion laptop and I was excited so I chipped my friend cufflinks on his boost and informed him that I just made a come up so if he wanted parts he needed to pick me up. Then I went into a deep thinking trance about how I was going to go about my day with the laptop so I decided that I had to get the stolen merchandise out of my possession. I approached the custodian that I sold marijuana to and demanded a trash bag. He looked puzzled so I repeated myself slowly and clearer, "GIVE ME A TRASH BAG" so he handed me a big clear one annoyed that I had moved him away from his cleaning cart and grabbed two extra thick black trash bags then I went to the bathroom and removed the laptop from my bag and placed it inside the trash bag. Knowing I couldn't walk around with a trash bag with stolen merchandise in it I walked towards the lockers remembering the movie ATL. I walked right past my assigned locker, went to an empty unassigned locker and placed the trash bag inside of it. I also had four other lockers with emergency equipment so I went to my emergency equipment locker, grabbed a new lock and locked up the stolen merchandise and remained calm for the rest of the day. When my last class was over I grabbed the trash bag with the laptop in it and proceeded to leave. As I was walking towards the door the school's police officer asked me what was in the trash bag. Thinking quickly on my feet I replied, "Shredded files from the principal's office." Then she nodded me off so I walked out the door. As I did, I saw Cufflinks with Chayo's green Saturn and I got in and took the ride down fifth street. I received four hundred dollars for the laptop. This became a weekly routine for me until the gravy train came to an abrupt stop.

One day the instructor who used that room on a regular basis noticed that out of the twenty -five boxes that used to contain laptops eight were empty. So, he instructed every platoon to get into formation in the cafeteria and made us do push-ups until someone told what happened to the equipment. No one ame forward. But, because of what happened, the room ecame off limits to everyone but the teachers. Every time I lade a come up in school, I called my right hand man Cufflinks or a ride to sell the merchandise and every time we included Vhiteboys older brother so we would all go get high on my ollar off of Xanax and exotic weed. After I realized I was lowing my money and had nothing to show for it, I chilled out or a small period of time and started going to the water tower 1 chestnut hill to increase the amount of clients. I had ventually come across three white teenage boys that were moking weed and I observed them until I knew which one 'as the alpha of their group. I could also tell from the aroma f the weed they were smoking that it was garbage so I walked ver to them and introduced myself as Hollywood Reese. Then pulled out a L that I had previously rolled up and told curious eorge to start smoking some real marijuana with me. At first e was hesitant so I lit it up, took a pull and blew the smoke in is face. Immediately he told his followers to put out the joint ney were smoking and pulled out ten dollars to buy my L. I ave him my number and told him whatever he was interested in more weed he could hit me up and he thanked me. We shook hands and I returned to my block. About an hour later he called me requesting a half ounce of what we smoked. I sold it to him seeing the lack of knowledge he had about Marijuana, I told him to meet me on my block with a hundred dollars in ten minutes. I didn't have that amount in my stash so I called my supplier and asked him to meet me on the block with a half-ounce. Curious George and his friends arrived earlier than I expected so I called my dealer to find out how long it was going to take him to show up. He gave me an estimated time of arrival of five minutes. Given his track record I knew that meant ten so I approached my new client told him to give me the hundred dollars and I'd be back in five I didn't want him to know I had to buy it from someone else so I took the money called up the connect and told him not to come because I was coming to him and I didn't want him to know I was playing the middleman for the transaction. I paid my connection fifty dollars for the half and I gave curious George his product. Then I had fifty dollars for myself. He asked me if I could get him some coke and I said of course, just let me know when and how luch. He thanked me and went about his business. That's then I discovered that making a profit off of being a middleman was the best role for me in the drug game.

he next day Curious George called me to buy three fifty pieces f coke and a dime of weed. I had the dime ready but I needed o grab three dubs that would pass for fifty pieces so I called ufflinks and asked him who he knew that had dubs of blow at could pass for fifties he directed me to this old head that urchased weed from him on a regular basis. I was surprised at I already knew dude when we met up this time and I didn't ave to play the I'll be back game. I paid for the three dubs myself and asked him if I could hit him up anytime for some he aid it was cool. Then I called Curious George back and told im to meet me on my block. He told me he was two minutes way so I met up with him, made the deal, and then it was onfirmed that I really knew I was that bull. The first time I made fifty dollars just off of knowing the right person and the econd time around I made one hundred because Curious eorge and his two friends called me every day for the same mount three fifty pieces of and a dime of weed. So I stuck to the script and continued making a hundred dollars a day and at the end of each day I'd put the hundred dollars up in a shoe box.

Everything was good until I slipped up after the fifth day. I used one day's profit to buy an eighth of coke which was only a hundred dollars so I still had four hundred tucked away. Because I was the middle man I didn't have anything to bag up the eighth so I hit up the old head that told me I could hit him up anytime and asked him for ten empties. He didn't have a problem with it so I picked them up and bagged up two hundred dollars in dubs. On the sixth day my cell didn't ring at all and I was really upset with myself for deviating from strictly being a middle man so I popped two Xanax to cheer me up. I thought I was going to be stuck with the ten dubs of coke for a while then my phone rang, and it was another client of mine, this bum ass old head that only bought dubs. I ignored his first call regretting the fact that Curious George wasn't my first play of the day. I guess the blues made me forget that I had dubs since I was strictly playing the middleman for a nice amount of time, so I called the client back and told him I was usy when he called. But I was available when he asked me to meet him on his block with two dubs.

fter I sold him what he wanted he informed me that his omie had pistols for one hundred eighty dollars. I told him I'd ink it over it and get back to him. I thought it over for a few ays and then I decided to take advantage of the deal so I called ull up so he could set up the deal. He gave me the man's umber and described what he looked like not wanting to eem too eager. I waited a while before I called but after an our, I finally called him and told me to meet him in front of e Papi store on Tulpehoken and Rodney. As I waited in front f the papi's, the man he described was walking towards me ith a plastic bag and I examined the shape of the bag which ad the appearance that a pistol was inside of it. he placed the ag on some steps near us and walked towards me then he aid your pistol is in that bag. Because the bag had the ppearance that a pistol was in it and he made the transaction eem really professional, I was comfortable with paying him. fter I handed him the 180$ I grabbed the bag as soon as I rabbed it, it felt way too light. That's when I knew I had gotten burnt. Pissed off I called Cufflinks and my uncle T, and I informed them on what just occurred. My uncle T told me his man A had a .44magnum bulldog for three hundred dollars. I told Cufflinks I only had one hundred and fifty dollars, so he put the other half up and now we had a pistol on deck.

I was still pissed off at the fact that I had got bamboozled so I decided to use the same scam dude did to me on someone else. That Monday when I returned to school, I began telling a select few that I had 9mm' for 200 dollars. Out of the three dudes I told one called me seven in the morning the next day asking if he could buy it before school. I told him yea and to meet me on the block next to the gas station. I grabbed one of those reusable shopping bags and started to fill it up. I put two broken cell phones, two hairbrushes, and a stone I found on my way to meet him inside the bag. The weight was perfect. When I got to the block, I told him to meet me. Then we began walking towards each other and I waited until he was ten yards away from me before I diverted and walked towards a set of steps. I put the bag down then I walked back over to him and nodded my head directing him towards the steps and xtended my hand to collect the two hundred dollars. After I ut the money in my pocket I briskly walked away, cut school, nd got high the rest of that day. I was surprised that he never alled to confront me about burning him that day. When I rrived at school the next day he didn't try to do or say nything to me. Little did I know he had a master plan up his leeve.

fter I made that come up, I bought an eighth of powder and a alf ounce of tree. I bagged up ten fat dimes with the half ounce f tree, five average size dubs, and four nice size dimes with 1e eighth back in school. I was still going about my business ke I didn't just make a new enemy, but I knew there was heat n my ass, so I started bringing only small amounts of drugs to ell in school. I downsized from bringing a bundle of weed and hundred dollars' worth of powder to only bringing three imes of weed and four dimes of powder. One morning before chool I met up with my homie DJ dust blaze who I normally kipped school with. We had intentions on cutting that day lso but as we walked around blowing some trees, he bought ff my connect, he reminded me that we were one unexcused absence from getting put on the truancy list. Not wanting to be one of those young bulls that got locked up for truancy, we decided to go after our third period class.

I approached one of the students that the guy I conned with the gun sold trees to and asked him if he was tired of sleeping on those small pillows that the bull, I burnt sold him. He replied, "Yeah why?" I reached into my shirt pocket, pulled out one of my husky dimes, grabbed his hand and said try sleeping on my pillows and his face lit up. That's when he remembered he was broke and said, "Sorry Moe I don't have twenty bucks." I laughed and said, "Dude you been fucking with the wrong people that's a dime." After he handed me the money for the bag, he said "Dude I'm only fucking with you on the weed tip from now on." So now not only did I con the student out of two hundred dollars, I also started stealing his clients. During lunch, the same student I just sold the dime to approached me and warned me that three students, snort face, hamburglar and yuck mouth all got caught smoking in the music room and that I should lay low for the rest of the day. Knowing I didn't sell them anything, his advice went in one ear and out the ther. The rest of the day went by nice and smooth until the 1st period.

Chapter 5

Caught Up

While I was asleep in the back of class with two dimes of weed in one shirt pocket and four dimes of coke in the other, the assistant principal entered the class requesting that I step into the hallway. As I stepped into the hallway, I saw two police officers standing outside her office and then I remembered that I had weed and on me, so I started fake coughing and said I needed water. Sliding off to the water fountain about twenty feet from her office where the cops were standing, I bent over, sipped some water and stuffed the weed down the drain. I completely forgot about the coke that I still had on me. As I stepped into the office, I saw a Ziploc bag with weed and aluminum foil in it then the officers entered the room and asked the three students if I was the one that sold them the weed. It took a minute to register that this was why the guy I conned that never said a word to me after I had gotten over on him. Each one of them looked teary eyed as they looked at me and said yes. My heart dropped to my knees. Knowing the drill, handed the officer closest to me my bag. Then his partner told

1e to empty my pockets. I took everything out of my pants

ocket. First all I had was a ten-dollar bill and my house keys.

hat's when I noticed that the pocket on my shirt was open

nd I remembered that I still had four dimes of powder inside.

o, I slightly turned away from the officer and swiftly reached

1 the pocket and balled the coke up inside my hand. Next, the

fficer told me to place my hands on the wall so he could

earch me. I moved towards the wall and stood as close as I

ould to the refrigerator that was in her office. While he

earched me, I slid my arm over the fridge and dropped the

oke behind it. Upset that he didn't find anything, he instructed

1e to take my shoes off and take out the soles. I did what he

sked and still coming up with nothing, he made a phone call

) the dean and informed her that the three kids that got

aught smoking had to be lying because all I had on me were

1y keys and ten dollars. She told him something that made

im more suspicious so he told me to come out the room with

im so we could talk. He stood in front of me to box me against

1e wall just in case I decided to run then he started acting like he was my friend. He asked if I got high that morning and if I ever sold drugs in the school. I answered *no* to all his questions and he told me some good news, he informed me that they were going to release me but because I was a minor, I needed my legal guardian to come sign the release form. That's when the dean's assistant walked down the hall towards us with a trash can, broom and mop. He spoke to the officer and asked if it was alright to start cleaning up the office. He was given permission to enter and started cleaning up. While doing this he found my coke and told the other officer that someone lost a pack of tokens. The cop stepped out and told his partner to place me under arrest and showed him the drugs I tried to hide while shaking his head in disgust. He walked me back into the office and cuffed me to a chair then called my mother.

I was put in the back of his squad car and a patty wagon was called for the other students. They put me in the juvenile holding cell and I had to wait three hours before I was processed, and my file sent downtown. I was there for a little more than twelve hours when my mom and aunt came to pick me up. I had to sign papers informing me of my court hearing that following morning. When my aunt dropped us off at the house, she straight up told me, "Stop fucking up!" then drove off. My mom began to tell me how upset she was with me and out the corner of my eye I noticed my brother creeping around the corner so he could sneak up on me. Without hesitation I started sprinting away. I ran out of my cadet shoes, burnt a hole in my sock, and skinned off my big toe. I sprinted from the front of our house all the way around the corner to the church field. Out of breath, I stopped running and tried to divert my brother's attention from me. Then our mom fell out in the middle of our driveway and he ran to help her up.

Due to all the chaos, my mom knew I couldn't stay the night without any disturbances occurring so she called one of her friends so I could spend the night and catch the bus to my preliminary hearing in the morning. I went over there exhausted and I fell asleep in a matter of minutes without any problems. The next morning my mom and I caught the bus to my preliminary hearing. By the time my case was called I already had my story straight. The woman that held the hearing read me and my mom the police report then asked my side of the story. I told her I was accused of selling narcotics to students in my school and was called out of class to be questioned and searched by the police. I told her how they searched my bag and my person, but no drugs were found then after I left the room narcotics were found while the three other suspects remained there. I swore to her that I never sold drugs in or out of school and she bought my story and agreed to dismiss the case. Once I completed my ten hours of community service and composed a letter about how drugs impacted my community, I thanked her and quickly exited the building. On the bus ride home, my mom told me that it was time for me to stop fucking around I agreed. But I disregarded her warnings immediately thereafter. To make matters worse, my mother received a call from my school telling her I wasn't allowed back on school property and that a unanimous decision was made that I would be attending a behavioral school called CEP Allegheny.

Later on, that day I went back in my stash and saw that I still had five dubs of coke. I took a black bandana out of my back right pocket which represented that I was a member of the lood gang but I was neutral. I caught the L bus down to Logan) sell some powder. While on the bus there was a skinny tall lack male with a pretty light skin proper thick female. They oth were wearing burgundy bandanas which indicated that ney were Piru blood gang members. He looked at me and said, Yo dawg! How you really feel about the blood brotherhood?" started a blood gang G-check sentence. G-checking is making ure the person is an official gang member. I recited the G-heck sentence *five popping... six dropping ...see a Crip kill a Crip ratch my favorite color drip*. He was like, "That's what it is omie." Then he started a conversation with me. He said "I otice you said what the Damu's say." *Damu* is Arabic for the rord 'blood'. He said, "Well me and my lady Piru bloods. I want ou to switch sets and change from your Damu set to our Vestside tree top Piru blood set." Then he invited me to a gang neeting so I could decide for myself. Afterwards I called my ig homie from the military academy which was also the lassmate that looked out for me when I stole that laptop. Due) our history he respected me and he approached me a few ays later telling me he told his gang leader about me and he authorized him to bless me in their gang. All I had to do was recite the oath.

I decided right then and there that I wanted to attend the Piru' gang meeting. I asked him to go with me to the gang meeting so we could see how the Piru bloods operated and he agreed to meet me at Broad and Olney. While preparing for the gang meeting I thought to myself *what am I going to do if Crips crash the meeting?* So I grabbed my .44 revolver and put on my red monkey shorts, my Nike T-shirt, and some black Chuck Taylors. I wore no bandana and no color of red. I chose not to wear any red because I didn't want to blend in with the other dudes that were going to be wearing all red. I also brought along some weed and met big homie at Olney. He had on a red Cincinnati fitted cap on. The cap had on it black letters CK which indicated the words *'Crip Killer'*. We caught the L train to 61st and market and then we went to Malcolm X park to smoke my weed and goof off.

When they arrived their set was small and only three members came to the meeting. Then the subject of me and my big homie

witching sets came up. My big homie said, "We respect
verything y'all are doing out here holding your part of West
hilly down but we're staying Damu to the grave." The Piru
ccepted how my big homie felt so we left Malcolm X park and
vent to one of their homes to watch the Eagles game but we
idn't realize that we were being watched the whole time.

he gang unit forces were taking pictures as we cut down
odman street. I noticed a fleet of squad cars zooming up the
lock so I made an about face and started walking in the
pposite direction down the street. I saw a group of men
itting on some steps near a row of parked cars and I
onchalantly walked over to the step closest to the cars. I
gured since I had on shorts I could let the gun drop from my
vaistline then kick it under one of the cars but the cops were
n point. I stood where I thought they couldn't see below my
vaist and reached down to make room for the gun to drop. As
oon as I did that they all pulled out their guns and demanded
nat I put my hands in the air. As soon as I did that the gun fell
nd each officer used their radio and yelled out, "MAN WITH A
UN, MAN WITH A GUN!" Then an Asian cop ran up on me and

forced me to the ground while jamming his knee in my back and placed the cuffs on me. He then placed me in the back of his squad car. I had my fake Temple I.D on me with the name ahmad Rashid and when he ran the name and discovered that it wasn't me, I lied and told him that the I.D was my cousins but I had stolen it from the security desk on campus so I could have access to the school and sell my coke whenever I wanted.

After I gave the officer my real information, I noticed the captain of the gang unit taking pictures of the four bloods that I was with and then the Asian cop drove me to the district. While at the district, the Asian cop was trying to handle me rough and trying to prove that he could handle my strength. I started resisting so he tried harder and he almost fell over when he tried to slam me against the wall. Another officer came around and said, "Keep it up and we'll add assault on an officer to your charge." So I chilled out and they put me in the juvenile holding cell. Although I didn't have anything red on me that afternoon, this slimy white officer takes a bandana from one of the Piru bloods and ties it to my .44 and they all try to trick me into signing for it with my property. It would've worked but I remembered my mother told me to always read the document before you sign it. After I read the words *red andana* I told them all I wasn't a dickhead and that I knew what they were trying to do so I crossed out the words red andana then signed the property sheet. Then this female officer said, "You look familiar. Do you have any family members on the force?" I told her my brother was officer Flowers. Then she asked me how I would like it if she called him up to her district and let him teach me a lesson. I told her no need for that. At midnight they shipped me to the Youth Study Center.

Chapter 6

Disgusting Decisions

I was assigned to the Honorable Judge Reynolds for my case and everybody felt sorry for me because he was known as a real stern Judge that gave out serious time. However by then I was a big time schemer and I managed to talk to the person in charge at Vision Quest and convinced him to allow my mother to bring a shirt and tie for my case by telling him, "The judge sees dozens of juveniles a day in institution issued clothes and I don't want to be looked at as a prisoner. I want him to see me as a young man aspiring for greatness." I also became cool with some important people that allowed me to compose a letter to the judge.

My Public Defender told me to tell the judge that I planned to move down south with my father but deep down I was also willing to take accountability by serving nine months of time. I knew that if I told the judge I was moving down south, he would've thought my frame of mind was that whenever I get in trouble I could just move to another state to get off. I thought lat wouldn't fly. So instead of going along with my nexperienced PD, I totally ignored his counsel, raised my hand nd said, "Your honor if I may, can I plead my own case to ou?" He said, "You're setting yourself up for failure but go head." I stood up straight and continued, "Judge Reynolds the nly thing I'm guilty of is being in the company of vicarious eople and all I want to do is finish school, enlist into the Air orce active Duty, make my mother proud and take care of my imily." He stopped and said, "Ok, case dismissed." He deferred djudication and released me on home monitoring. The istrict Attorney said, "Your Honor this is absurd he is a threat o the commonwealth of Pennsylvania! His record clearly hows that he's a menace to society." Judge Reynolds said, This isn't going to be another win notch on your belt. We're ilking about a young man's life. I don't care Blood, Crip gang, r no gang. This is a young man that wants to serve his country s I did so I'm letting him go so he can achieve his goals." Then e looked at me and said, "You didn't know I did twelve years f active duty in the Air force. Only thing is you're not as handsome as I was when I enlisted." I laughed at his lame ass joke knowing I was getting off on house arrest.

I got a ride home with my mom from two of her friends. It turns out that the home monitoring officer was all the way on-point because she knew that I would mess up. I wasn't home for no longer than twenty minutes before she arrived at my house to set up the equipment. She instructed me that I couldn't tie up the line for no longer than thirty minutes and that I could go outside but not on the sidewalk. The following Monday I enrolled into CEP Allegheny. I got my girlfriend to call the school as my mother so I could get out early on Tuesdays and Thursdays. Eventually I got bored with the mundane learning environment so I dropped out and acquired my GED. Not too long after that I received some bad news.

Before the gang episode occurred I received a call with a Sergeant recruiter for the Air force about me enlisting. But, because I didn't graduate with a high school diploma, I was pushed to the bottom of the deployment list for Air force basic training. Then I met SGT Vastag, a recruiter for the U.S Army, nd he made me retake the ASVAB. I passed with a fifty four

en my recruiter sent me to MEPS out Fort Dix. MEPS is the

edical examination for the military. I passed the HIV/STD

est, the drug test, and I passed everything else but when the

octors asked me what happened to my neck and ear because

ere's two very noticeable scars in appearance. When I was

fteen I had gotten hit in the back of my head with an forty

unce glass beer bottle. BecauseI was scared that if I told them

hat really happened they would've disqualified me for gang

ffiliation, I decided to lie and said I had the scars since I was

toddler. I told them that I ran through a glass door and got

wo deep cuts. The doctor was suspicious and thought I had a

etal eardrum so they temporarily disqualified me until they

eceived proof that I didn't have a metal eardrum.

never showed any proof and eventually I just gave up but SGT

astag never gave up on me. He stayed in contact with me

forming me that there was something special about me and

at whenever I was ready to come around he'd be there for

e. He also told me that I had what it took to become an

xcellent soldier.

Before all of this occurred I experienced a dumb situation with the college dudes from the Temple campus that I stole the I.D card from. They invited me to a Temple party and I wanted to really enjoy the party so I purchased twelve Xanax pills and I popped two of the pills then smoked a joint of haze before we left. Xanax can alter your mood easily and after we smoked my phone started freezing out of nowhere and it kept saying *please restart your mobile device* so I pressed restart plenty of times but the phone didn't do anything. I was high and annoyed so I threw the phone against the wall twice and then I stomped it until it was really broken. Then I started talking to it like the phone could actually understand me saying *"See what happens when you mess with real nigga you piece of shit phone!"* I had to re-up my stash and had a little money on me that night, four one hundred dollar bills. I placed the ten remaining Xanax inside of the plastic Dutch wrapper and left the house.

At the party, this chick from D.C. with this fat ass kept putting the moves on me while crushing my drugs in my pocket. I grabbed her by her waist and said, "Damn shorty calm down ou're crushing my pills." She said, "You don't need to be opping any pills anyway." Then she started throwing her ass ack even harder. I gently pushed her off me and pulled out ıy plastic Dutch wrapper and noticed all my pills were now in owder form. I became pissed and decided to swallow all the owdered Xanax. It tasted really nasty so I stumbled over to ıe drink table and asked how much for a drink. The pretty ᵊmale said it cost two dollars. So I pulled off two bills. If you otice I said *bills* and not *dollars.* After I paid the lady, she left ıe drink on the table and then I blacked out but I don't ᵊmember for how long. But, when I came out of it I was ehind the table pouring my own drinks. Niggas started ice rilling me so I lifted up my shirt showing I was strapped and ll the niggas that were ice grilling me stopped.

hen my college friends told me to go out with them and I was lasted out of my mind. The D.C chick was giving me that pecial look and I thought she wanted me to give her the usiness so I asked them for five minutes alone. When I finally ot outside I noticed the car wasn't there so I figured my five ıinutes had expired but I wasn't about to start walking around North Philly at three in the morning high and alone looking for them. So I stood at the light on Broad and Susquehanna. When it went from red to green, I blacked out again. When I became alert, I found myself sitting on the bench at the bus depot across the street from the Cheltenham mall with the glare from the sun burning my eyelids. It was now one in the afternoon. I was surprised that I still had my gun and the rest of the money on me. This is exactly why you should never experiment with narcotics. I could've gotten robbed and killed that night. I got change for a hundred dollar bill and then caught the bus to the college crib. I didn't even knock, I just barged inside stormed upstairs and started looking for the nigga that drove us because he left me. But a nigga named John Sport was the only one home and he explained how I was drawlin the other night. He then calmed me down and I put twenty dollars on his desk and said sell me ya boost. With no argument he handed me the boost.

Chapter 7

Breathing Underwater

Vinter approached fast, everybody was grabbing drugs to get poppin' so they could ball in the summer. My ol' head Gub grabbed a quarter pound of weed and bagged up these husky nickel bags that were the size of dime bags. He wanted me to get it poppin on his little cousin's block so I graduated from cocaine to crack. One day we were standing on Franklin and Pike and Gub started yelling "Trees out! Trees Out!" He handed me an empty potato chip bag filled with his product. It was a hundred dollars worth and he told me to just bring back eighty dollars. I told him it wasn't a problem but thinking to myself *I'm selling these Uptown as dimes, fuck feeding the block.* I chilled down F&P for about two more hours and had a business talk with Gub's cousin. He explained how he got his corner then explained how he ran his corner and showed me where they stashed their guns. He even offered me a bullet head's shift on his corner but I refused that night and told the bullet head that it was too hot down there so we should roll out and come grab a pack on a different day. While Uptown I sold my three white boys these fat nickel bags as dimes. The weed was some fire and I sold both of them five bags each. I was doubling Gubs money but he knew I was selling them as dimes and didn't mind because my cousin K called to tell me this.

Gub had some ten milligram Percocets but he didn't have any clientele so I told him about the dude's corner and said a bunch of Ricans were always down there looking for all types of shit. I hit the dude up on his cell and told him *I was ready*. He knew what that code meant. When we got down F&P this fresh ass nigga had on a Gucci t-shirt, Gucci loafers, and a Gucci bucket hat.

They exchanged numbers and he shook my hand passing me off one hundred and forty dollars worth of crack cocaine all in nickel bags. He had that really potent product. Afterwards I walked to eighth and Bristol grabbed me a dime of wet and a strawberry blunt. I called up Trini and told D I was on my way down. I called him because Hutchinson street already had flow of base heads and I was planning an all-nighter to sell roduct around there. I called my mom and lied to her telling er I was at my cousin Jeffreys house in Jersey for the night nd she believed me. D told me that if I wanted to start up a ow, give the base head he knew a tester and he would spread le word. So I listened and gave the base head one rock. The lan worked and he went and told everybody. Business lasted off after that. I fell asleep in the front room down in the asement but I didn't stay asleep for long because all night rack heads were knocking on the window of that room /anting a fix. D said, "Moe you drawin' having all these rackheads on my lawn!"

y this time I was dumb high so I asked him what time was. He old me it was midnight and I asked him to take over but I lade the after hour prices double. He sold all the nickels for imes and I broke him off with a nice little piece of change. I ave Gub the hundred dollars to give to his cousin for the bean orty pack he gave me to sell. He tried to slick talk me by aying, "MOE why don't you give my cousin some of that extra loney you made. D told me what ya'll did with the work that night." Trying to further convince me he said, "All the extra money you give him is put in a bail money box in-case you get booked." I said, "NO I'm keeping my bread!" After that bullet head hustled two packs down the bull block but bull tricked him a different way by telling him to give him back the whole profit and get paid on Thursday.

He did it like a dick head. Since he was a young bull clocking ten different corner boys and collecting hundreds of dollars every hour, you know he wasn't going to remember his little eighty dollars. He sold out two packs that day and he went for that bullshit.

Bullet head asked me to catch the bus down to the bull block so he could grab his eighty bucks, some packs, and some wet. I went with him and when he asked the bull for his pack money, the bull said *what money.* Bullet head was ready to pop off on bull but I told him to chill because there were at least four shooters watching his ass and he refused me a pack because he heard I was making double off his work. Then I remembered that I had met this bull before when Gub's rother introduced me to him and when I started thinking

where and who introduced me to him, it came to me that it was

ub's brother, called Monday. Since bull said he would only

ell weight to his family, I got Monday to start grabbing for me

uarter ounces and halves but each time I had to grease

Monday's palm with five or ten dollars just to get the work. I

nked up with Chayo and Cufflinks when it came to selling

ard and we hustled on these other bulls block because our

riend Trini lived on that block. We felt as though because she

ved there, it gave us the right to grind down there. I hollered

t the base head that D introduced me to and he blasted off in

 corner twenty feet from where I was standing. Extremely

nsatisfied, he asked me what I sold him. I responded, "That's

hat butta me and my team whipped up." He laughed and said

Butta no sir I want them dimes you had when we first met

hat was the real deal." So I started back greasing Mondays

alms just to grab more work for me off the bull block.

We were all some wet heads. When I got high off PCP I felt

motionless I did whatever I wanted to do and to whoever I

elt like doing it to. I didn't have a conscience. I started stealing from everybody's cell phones, electronic devices, anything that was worth money.

After a few months, I got a job at UPS out Willow Grove mall. My associate, Little Rock, worked there as an unloader and I was a loader. He put me down on how he tripled his checks while on the job. It turns out, after every work shift he would steal phones, iPod's, and anything he could get his hands on that was worth money. He told me the female security guard was a real hard ass and she was constantly trying to find something stolen on him. Since I was tall and handsome, I decided to charm her. Every day I would compliment her and joke around asking when she was going to allow me to take her out to eat. After a while it got to the point that she stopped using the portable metal detector wand on me but I still had to walk through the one that was inside the booth where every employee had to exit. I asked little rock how he got past the metal detector with the merchandise. He unzipped his pants and showed me he was wearing jeans and sweatpants. I was now down with how to get away with burning the company for merchandise. I decided to purchase a pair of real baggy

tate property jeans and it was on and popping from that point
n.

started snatching four cell phones a day but they were just
our typical cell phones. I was snatching the phones that were
eing returned to the company because something was wrong
/ith them. I tried to sell the phones to the store owners in my
eighborhood as if they worked normally but quickly
iscovered they were all defective so he only paid me twenty
ve per cell and I made an extra hundred after every shift. I
lso got my homie John Sport a gig there.Then on my
hristmas eve shift I already had an agreement with the shift
upervisor that every day at 5:30pm I could clock out because
ιe last bus came at 5:45pm. He conveniently forgot about our
greement and told me I had to stay until 6pm I asked him if
e was going to drive me home and he said "NO!" so I left and
aught my bus on time leaving with two blackberries and two
-Mobile razor phones.

he next day I went in for my shift and I was told that I was
red for walking out on the job. I guess Sport was trying to

prove he was loyal to me because I got him the job and he wanted to quit. I told him he didn't have to quit just because they fired me. He was like, "Naw fuck them G we out!" Pissed off, I went home and started looking for another job. It seemed like every job I applied for did drug screening and background checks. I was at a dead end because my urine stayed dirty and my criminal background had aggravated assault with a firearm violation on it so nobody wanted to hire me.

I was in a low state of mind and feeling useless in life. I became depressed so I continued getting high every day and night smoking three dipsets a day and popping eleven Xanax. I was a walking Zombie and I smelled like a human chemical. My uncle D was the main advocate in my life supplying me with free get highs. I gladly accepted every dipset and every pill he offered. My brother was constantly coming at my neck trying to snap me out of my drug addiction but like most addicts I was blinded and taken hostage mentally by narcotics. The Wet I smoked messed me up pretty bad but it was the Xanax that really turned me out. After I popped four I felt like I could do anything in the world. I would look for houses that appeared o have valuable merchandise inside and then climb up a tree losest to a window on the house and scale on the edge of the indow. Then I would force open the window, slip inside their ouse, and just steal from the home. Nobody was ever there hen I did my breaking and entry but then I crossed the line nd back stabbed my brother.

one crusher and I smoked three dipsets to the face and lacked out in his room. All I could see was purple and green treams of light and the entire room started to spin. I threw up i my mouth six times then I stumbled nine blocks to my ouse. I barely got up to my room. I was extremely hot and hirsty so I stripped naked and made my way down to the itchen to grab some soda. With my bare ass in the efrigerator I heard footsteps coming towards the kitchen. It irned out to be my brother. He stepped into the kitchen and I ecame embarrassed and grabbed the roll of paper towels to over up my manhood. He snapped on me asking what the fuck as I doing naked in the fridge. I quickly forgot that I took all iy clothes off and I replied, "Huh, I am?" He shook his head ith disgust and told me to go upstairs and stay in my room until the next day. I scurried up to my room and the following morning my mom cursed me out for not respecting our household. I didn't see any issue because I was still completely spaced out. My addictions had completely taken over my mental capacity.

Chapter 8

On the Run

didn't learn my lesson. I came up with a plan to steal my rothers .357 smith and Wesson snub nose revolver so I pread a rumor telling every homeowner I knew in my eighborhood that there were some drug addicts going round breaking into homes. After I told a good ten omeowners, I decided it was time to make my move. On the ay I decided to carry out my plan I woke up still high from the ight before and I told my brother the same rumor I told the ther people. He said he knew already so I waited for him to ave for work. Immediately after I heard his vehicle pull out f the driveway, I used a butter knife to get past the lock on his oor. Then I started my search and for the first twenty minutes couldn't find anything. Then I started rearranging things and mistakenly knocked over his laundry basket. His .44magnum esert eagle fell on the floor and I quickly put it inside my ocawear winter coat pocket.

I rushed down to Cufflinks house to show him the score but he didn't think it was a good idea to steal from my combat bound brother. He still found me a buyer and his plug traded me 2000 dollars worth of marijuana for the .44 magnum desert eagle. Later that afternoon my mother called my cell but already knowing what the call was about I ignored the first four calls. By the fifth call I was ready to hear what she had to say but when I answered I heard a ruffling noise and it was my brother grabbing the phone from our mom. His first words were "I know you did this but I'm going to give you one chance to return my gun and I won't touch you or call the cops but if you don't I can reassure you that you won't have to worry about running from the law because I'm coming straight for you after we hung up." I hit my homie up from South West Philadelphia requesting a place to hideout and he provided a place out 51st and Hazel. Needing to make some money before I skipped town, I grabbed some baggies and bagged up 1200$ in dimes and $800 in dubs. My mother called me to come collect my belongings so I got the bull's baby mom to drive me to my mom's house to grab my stuff. She had every single item of line packed. Sitting in the car while my homie and his girl grabbed my things, I saw my brother writing down the tag number and he had his cell in his hand. They saw he was very agitated so they quickly got my stuff in the van then I gave them each twenty dollars and asked to be dropped off downtown. I had too much stuff to carry so I asked them to hold most of my things until I got back. That turned out to be a big mistake. While on the run, I received three calls from cufflinks but I ignored the first two and answered the third. He called to inform me that our homie was returning to Atlanta for school and she was driving. He recommended that I hitch a ride with her and get dropped off in D.C where we had connections. So I called her up to see if I could ride. By this time everybody was looking out for me and she agreed. On the ride down she asked me what happened and why was I in a rush to get to D.C. I lied and told her someone broke into my house and stole my brothers guns and he was blaming me.

Only my mom and three friends knew I was going to D.C to hide out and I decided to hide out in Prince George county where I started selling ounces for $90. I would line my briefs up with three ounces at a time and stand in-front of Danny's Chinese store and trap in P.G. County where the dealers normally sold ounces of medium grade for $125. But, I wanted to step on toes and crush the competition so I sold mine for less. I sold two ounces every time I went to Danny's and the dude I was squatting in a house with had a lot of friends that wanted to take advantage of my prices. I got him to juice up the situation by telling them that my low price would only be around for one weekend because I was going back up north real soon which was false because I needed to stay away from Philadelphia as long as I could.

By the second week I was out of town, I received a call from a detective from the thirty fifth district. I was high and paranoid and could not control my temper so I snapped on him and shouted that there wasn't any physical evidence linking me to my brother's robbery. He replied, "Be that as it may if it wasn't you why did you leave the state?" I told him I was willing to come back to PA whenever he wanted me to. He said, "Alright so I'll see you Monday right?reg' aining my composure I respectfully said "Yes sir." When Monday arrived I caught the hina bus straight to New York skipping PA because I didn't

ust getting off in Central Philadelphia. I didn't know if my

olks tipped the PPD off or if they gave the police my phone

umber so what was stopping them from not telling them how

was returning? I caught the China bus straight to N.Y then got

ack on arriving in Philadelphia. When I arrived my pupils

vere irregular due to me smoking four to five L's a day while

1 P.G county. I went back Uptown to the college dudes house

o prepare for my arrest. I fronted my lil homie two ounces

lready bagged up because he was like family and I only

equested $120. Then I went to my uncle T and left him with

vo ounces. I also told him I was going to give him the same

eal Cufflinks always gave me. I called it a husband and wife

eal, two ounces for $150. He agreed and I asked him to hold

n to the four ecstasy pills that I had bought in P.G. county.

Iy mother didn't want me wandering the streets so she called

iy girlfriend A dub to put me in a hotel for a few nights. My

rst night in the hotel I relaxed and blew four L's to the face

nd in the morning I went to the district looking for the

letective. He wasn't there the first four times I went but my mother thought I was lying so she accompanied me the fifth time. Another Detective confirmed that the Detective I was looking for really wasn't there and my mother asked him if he could take over since the detective that was overseeing the case was never there. He tried but after seeing the files on the case he refused in a polite and respectful manner. He told us that he didn't want to interfere with a case that he wasn't there from the beginning for. My mother asked him to call the Detective that I was supposed to be questioned by and get a date and time that he was going to be there so we could move forward instead of standing still. The Detective did what my mother asked and scheduled an interrogation the following Thursday at nine am. Unfortunately my mother had to work that day and the Detective twisted all my words around in her absence. He took me being respectful and chill about the situation as me being nonchalant about stealing from my brother. However that was far from the truth. My mother had raised me to always be respectful no matter how enraged I became which was something I could do effortlessly as long as I was sober. But when I was high off of one of the many drugs was abusing, I couldn't control my rage and I easily became rovoked and would snap when the questioning began. He ied to deceive me at first showing me a marked up piece of aper with finger prints from my brother's gun case on it and e said that they were my fingerprints. I knew he was bluffing ecause I never touched the gun case. All I did was look under ie mattress and under the entire bed and then the dresser rawers. After I did all of that I trashed the room and while I as trashing the room that's when I mistakenly knocked over ie laundry basket and found the firearm.

lthough I was guilty as sin, I offered to take a polygraph test ecause someone taught me how to cheat the test. But the etective said he wasn't going to waste taxpayers money on an pen and shut case. Then he went on to explain he knew I was ing because I was too mild tempered. He went to ask a ifferent detective a question and but whatever he asked ealed the deal on my arrest. That's when he turned back wards me and said, "You're full of shit! Stand up and put your ands behind your back. You're under arrest for the theft of fficer Flower's firearm." Then they took me to the juvenile holding cell. When I arrived inside the juvenile holding cell there was this middle eastern juvenile in custody for DUI. I couldn't even take a seat on the bench because he was asleep and urinating all over himself. I tapped his sneaker asking him to wake up. After he got up, I told him to get some paper towels and spray from the cops so he could spray and wipe down the bench. Then I sat down and relaxed because I knew I was going to be there for a while. I sat there waiting throughout the day and about half a dozen juveniles were placed under custody. I was there until one in the morning and then transferred to the Youth Study Center again.

Since this was my third time there, I already knew all the staff members. After the first day I had an interview to determine whether I was eligible for release or not. Their rules made it mandatory that any juvenile that had a firearm violation wasn't eligible for release. I pretty much knew I wasn't going to be released back upstairs so I grabbed a sci-fi novel and read all three hundred and fifty pages in two hours. Then a CBS coordinator came to interview me to see which facility would be best for me. That night, he assigned me to Vision Quest and was transferred. I arrived at ten pm and I was assigned to ʋing-D. When I arrived, everyone in the wing was staring at ɪe. I went to hut number five but because I wasn't medicated, couldn't fall asleep so I just held my breath until I passed out ɪe next morning.

woke up to two juveniles slap boxing in my hut. Once I bserved everyone in my hut were some playful young bulls, I ecided to stay out of the way. I requested to switch huts since already knew all the staff and they allowed me to switch. The ays went by without me getting into any altercations but that uickly changed when this skinny short Hispanic male was put ɪ my wing. I hadn't noticed he had been observing my actions nd he approached me and said, "I noticed you're the only bull one of these other dickheads mess with." I said, "Ok what do ou want from me?" He said, "I just want you to look out in xchange for anything like pills, Newport's, weed, food, nything." I was like, "Bet you have a deal! I'll look out for ou for a pack of ports and all your trays every day but you an keep your snacks." After a week of him giving me all his ·ays in exchange for agreeing to look out for him, nothing happened until one day this tall black Lamar Odom looking dude was placed in our wing. I he would always start talking to me about how we should form an alliance and take control of the unit because we were the biggest. I told him I wasn't there to take over and I was simply trying to stay out the way until my case got dismissed. He had no choice but to respect how I felt but I could tell from his facial expression that his plans to take over the unit were going to continue with or without me.

The next week at chow I noticed the look in the Hispanic kid's eyes. I saw he was hungry and everyone witnessed him give me his trays daily. I wanted to make sure he didn't try to say I forced him to give up his trays so   I passed him off three oranges and told him to tuck them in his pants. I specifically told him not to put them in his socks but he didn't listen. As the whole D-wing walked back to the unit, one of the staff members noticed him with oranges in his tube socks. He took the oranges and instructed him to do thirty pushups and ordered me to do fifty. I knocked out the fifty pushups in no time then the staff member returned his attention to the

panish bull and demanded the thirty pushups. He said, "Fuck
o! Eat a dick." After that remark the staff bull said alright
ghts out at 6pm instead of 9pm and everyone was enraged.
he main staff that was cool didn't have much to say. While in
ıe hut with the Spanish bull, Slinky and DJ were all cool then
ıe Spanish bull asked if he could use the restroom. One staff
ıember said, "No piss on yourself thieving ass youngbull."
hats when the the Hispanic bull flipped him off.

he staff bull that said it was cool and because everybody
roke their necks trying to prove their loyalty to him,
veryone from hut number one asked him what did he want
ıem to do about that disrespect. In reply he shrugged his
houlders and said *do what y'all want.* Then six juveniles
ushed to my hut. I stopped them at the entrance and said,
Γhis is my hut! Fuck what yall trying to prove. Nobody is
oming to my house to do anything!" The ones that heard
bout the story of me breaking the kids jaw in middle school
rith a single punch just walked away but the Lamar Odom
ɔoking juvenile from eighteenth and Diamond didn't care
bout what I did in middle school. He ran up and threw a jab

trying to chin check me as I leaned back avoiding the punch, but it landed in my chest immediately. I rushed after him but the cool low key staff guard grabbed me by my waist. I had no idea a skinny short bull like him could hold me back. After hearing all the ruckus that was going on, the big bad 6"9 350 lbs.' chief on duty came and gripped the bull up and tossed him into the wall. Then told this other sloppy fat staff dude to escort us into the hallway. A staff member told us to stand up straight against the wall and the whole time i was mean mugging him but he was too afraid to look me in my eyes but I was still hawking him down anticipating my revenge for the hit he landed on me.

Big boss called him over before me and I waited for him to walk in front of me before I reacted. I attacked him with two hooks to the body and four straight jabs to his left eye then a kidney shot. The staff yelled code black over their walkie talkies which meant a disturbance was in process Big Boss told the staff member from Haines St. to escort me and bull back to D-wing. I overheard the dickhead say, "This ain't over I promise you that." When I got back to the wing, everybody in ny hut was acting like chicks and asking me every detail. I told them to be cool because I really didn't mind but after lights out. During lights out, if you're caught talking or eating the staff makes you pull your cot to the middle of the Wing. Fortunately the juvenile I just attacked was running his mouth about how their whole hut was going to rush into my hut to jump me after everybody fell asleep.

After his dumb ass got caught, he had to move his cot in the middle of the unit so I strategically ducked into the corner of my hut where no one could see me. After I was concealed, the big Boss man asked the dickhead bull to take the water cooler out of the unit. It was an open opportunity to react to the comment he made about our feud not being over but I had to be patient and wait for the big boss man to leave. After he left there was still a staff member in the unit but I was very provoked and determined to blacken both his eyes. I heard his footsteps getting closer so I sprinted straight at him. He tried tossing the cooler at me to slow me down but the attempt failed because my reflexes from football practice as a middle linebacker were still on point. I deflected the water cooler then I gripped the back of his neck so I could control which direction the fight went. After I started throwing some serious punches to his head and body the beat down lasted about ninety seconds and then Haines ST. ran up behind me and scooped me up. He slammed me onto the floor then put me in a choke hold. He had an extremely tight grip around my neck with his arm. My eyes started rolling to the back of my head and I started tapping out. After he noticed I was on the verge of passing out, he released me out of the choke hold. Afterward the overweight staff member that was on watch grabbed me by my ankles and dragged me into the hallway. He was so furious that he banged my head against the door and chipped my front tooth. The boss wanted to write me up for the altercation but another staff member, Monty, vouched for me by telling the big boss man what the Lamar Odom looking Juvenile said. Before they let us back on the unit, the big boss man tore up the incident slip and had me moved to A-wing where I received another call from my recruiter telling me that Friday morning I was going back to MEPS because that's when they moved my court date to. During my court hearing, my iom and my brother were there. My brother stood up and aid if my brother is ready to turn his life around by joining the .S army then I'm willing to drop all charges. The next week I ras released.

Chapter 9

Second, Third, and Fourth Chances

I knew that I couldn't go back to my home so my loving mother made arrangements for me to stay with my folks on Dorset st. I had a hell of a lot of fun my first night there. My cousin's fiance said "You thirsty young buck?" knowing he wasn't talking about your typical beverage I said, "Yea, what's good?" In reply he said, "What's good is this half ounce of prometh I'm about to give you. I was too excited and ready to get my lean on. He handed me the cup and I got off the sofa bed to sipped my purple with him. After I drank half of the half ounce he pulled out five dollars and said here go grab a box of vanilla Dutch's. This ol' head stayed on his lean and he'd fall asleep in the middle of a cypher with the L burning holes in his shirt. Whenever this happened, everybody in the cypher would just start laughing the whole time. While living there I was allowed females in my room but as far as drugs went, I only paid for Dutch's no weed, pills, or lean. The owner of the house said that she owned a 9mm pistol and warned me that

I stole that like I stole my brother's she wouldn't drop any charges. I reassured her that I wouldn't steal not one red cent from them. After I got settled in I wanted to go out with my ex but everyone recommended I stay in so I wouldn't cross my brother's path. As a conciliation the owner said I could have females over whenever I wanted. Knowing how I always took things too far, after someone gave me an inch I took a mile and ruined that freedom. My area was the basement and I didn't respect those boundaries so then I had to go.

My mother was a hairdresser and she knew everybody. With nowhere to go she called her former co-worker to see if I could bunk there for a little while. I had to share a room with her son and he wasn't happy about that. Every chance he got he constantly complained to his mother about me crowding his space. Around this time I started hanging out with these other white boys. I constantly conned them because they would say that there was a touch of purple on the leaves so I told them it was haze and started selling twenties for forty or whatever amount they wanted. I charged them double. After a few weeks of me serving the white boys, they offered to sell me a more potent type of haze. After realizing they cocked my pistol for me I told them I wanted a quarter pound and they informed me that it'll be eleven hundred dollars. Since I was always looking for a come up, I agreed on the price so I started thinking about what approach I was going to take. Then I decided to hit him with the fifty four fake out but a car was necessary to carry out my plan. I wasn't driving at the time but I remembered most of my homies that drove usually went to Finley rec center to smoke so that' where I decided to go. I had a good feeling I was going to run into somebody I knew that was down for the move I wanted to make when I arrived at the rec center I was pleased to see that gut served me right so I approached the trips and asked which one of them wanted two ounces of haze in exchange for a five minute ride the oldest didn't trust me after hearing so many stories about the cons I pulled on people in the past the middle one felt the same way so my last hope was the youngest one swift he didn't care about the stories or the people I conned he just wanted to know where we had to go with everything in order I made the call and set up the deal we agreed to meet at the gas station fter he got off of work which was around nine thirty so me

nd trip just relaxed and went over how we were going to get

im for the package so I explained to him how the fifty four

ike out works he doubted that it would work and started

iving me suggestions for a more effective approach each one

f his suggestions involved excessive violence I shook my head

nd told him he watched too many movies that' when I

ecided to just go with the flow and told him to follow my lead

hen we met up to make the exchange he had someone with

im so I got in their car inspected the package questioned if it

as one hundred and twelve grams and told them I need to

eigh it before I gave them the money the driver then reaches

n his glove box and hands me a pocket scale I laughed at him

nd said are you serious that' what you use to weigh the

eight you sell he said yeah why I explained to him that the

ntire package has to be placed evenly on to the scale in order

o get an accurate measurement he looked at me as if I wasn't

upposed to know that and suggest I ride with him to

oylestown so we can weigh it I told him I have an extra-large

cale at my trap house just up the block then he told me to

show him the way I acted like I was offended and snapped saying what you think I'm a fucking amateur I'm not showing you shit and told his partner to get in the Car with me to weigh it before I got out his car I stuffed the quarter pound of haze under my jacket and walked to swift' car I got in before the white boy did so I tucked the package under the seat and told swift to stay cool and follow my lead then the white boy got in so I told swift to drive to the trap we drove up the street pulled over I told them both I'd be back after I weighed it so I cut through the house stand in the drive way for a minute then called swift and told him to put bull on the phone he said yeah what's up everything cool with the plan in motion I snap and told him it was short 16 grams then told him to come see for himself after I heard the car door shut I cut through another house further up the driveway swift pulls up laughing his ass off when I got in he asked where was the package and if I took any out I told him to stop acting like his brothers and that it was under the seat I couldn't take him to my cousin' house to split the come up and his mom was home so I called my cousin' fiance and told him I needed to break

omething down he told me to come through as long as I was
oing to look out so I told swift where to go when I got out the
ar with the large brown paper bag my cousin' fiance told me
nd swift to keep the noise down because my cousin mom was
leep and we went in the house and weighed out four ounces i
anded swift the two I promised him then we both gave ol'
ead a nice amount for letting us use the house I asked him to
ell his people' that I had quarter ounces of haze out for one
undred twenty five dollars so he made some calls and helped
ie sell three quarters that night the next day I got swift to
rive me to grab some jars so I could sell twenties and fifties,
ieanwhile back at my little cousin' house

e was getting messed with while he was hustling so I decided
) post up at his trap with him he had this girl as a customer
re went to school together it was late and I wanted to bone so
asked him to step aside he was pissed but knew what game I
ras playing even though I just got some yams earlier that
ay I wanted more so I approached her asked how much she
ranted showing off I gave her twice as much she said that it
ras too much so I told her to blow half with me she agreed so

I grabbed a Dutch and a condom confident that it was about to go down. I told her I knew a little ducky spot where we could blow peacefully and after we finished smoking I seduced her. We got in the back seat and we rocked out but I wasn't comfortable in the yacht at all so I pulled out of her and removed the condom and went back in. Now I was cool. After we finished I had her drop me off on the corner of my cousins block. When I got inside I asked his mother if there was anything she needed me to do and I helped her out.

Over the next few days me and swift drove around selling our haze. I even stopped getting wetted so I could save my money and find a spot of my own but I knew that just selling weed wasn't going to get me the money I needed. I walked to the McDonalds down the street from his house and asked if they were hiring. The manager informed me about the job fair they were having that weekend and I was happy that I was about to start back working. That Saturday I arrived a half hour early for the job fair and I applied for the overnight position, nine at night to seven the next morning. After reading my resume and seeing that I had experience in the fast food industry, I was ired on the spot. I decided I was going to put my best foot orward while working there and I was doing pretty good too. hen the girl my cousin sold the tree to called my phone to tells le she was pregnant and I gave her an std. I was scared out of ly mind and I asked her to describe her symptoms. The next lorning I rushed straight to the free clinic on Chelten avenue. Vhen I got called to see the doctor, I told her I recently had sex nd the girl said I gave her an std and told her the symptoms le girl was having. She checked my penis for inflammation nd foreign discharge. Then she explained to me that the girl rho claimed I gave her an std most likely had a yeast infection nd wasn't aware. I asked her how she figured I gave her omething and she explained that most teenage women don't se the right products to cleanse themselves. I gave a urine ample and the nurse drew some blood to check for hiv and ther stds. It took five days for me to get the results which eemed like forever and I was a nervous wreck. I started eleting numbers of random girls out of my phone because I rasn't taking any more chances. When I received the call that was clean I was filled with joy.

During this time I was still living at my cousins house and my mom told me that if I get a secondary education she'd hook me up with a place of my own to call home. I hurried up and searched the web for trade schools and I found Strayer University but it wasn't in my community and I damn sure couldn't afford a dorm room so I chose Lincoln tech in center city for pharmacy technician. I had perfect attendance every module and a 3.7 gpa. I really never had to study, my entire middle school years I got straight A's and B's on my report card without ever opening a book to study. I did the same while attending Lincoln tech. My mother hooked my new pad up with a 42 inch LG plasma flat screen and 20 inch desktop and all my furniture was Italian leather.

Now that I had my own headquarters I could run things how I wanted. I immediately linked up with my homie Havoc because I remembered observing him and his squad making moves. They always switched their cars up and I would be in my driveway real late with my uncle T. We would see Havoc and his squad changing clothes. My uncle once told me they were robbing dudes. I still decided to call Havoc up for a usiness discussion and we talked about how we would perate. We made up rules for our squad and called ourselves ie Body Snatchers. Some of our rules were no women, no egulars, only do business with mainly heroin dealers and ocaine dealers. We only jammed one weed dealer. We were nown as the body snatchers because we snatched dealers up nd took their stash. I mainly did the enforcing but did no tabbing or shooting, just heavy left hooks and some serious traight jabs. We never had to intimidate the prey for longer ian twenty minutes because I'm a heavy hitter. After our first core I treated myself to a 96 Cadillac Deville and three iousand dollars in clothes. It was all exclusive stuff. I also had 500 dollars in weed bagged up in husky nicks then divided ie 1500 into 15 hundred dollar packs. I stretched that 5000 ollars as long as my extravagant life allowed. The only thing ; I was sloppy and left evidence all over my pad and my mom ould bug out. However I didn't allow any wet smoke in my ad. If you smoked that you had to step out back in the riveway.

When it was time for me to graduate from Lincoln Tech, I realized that I was bamboozled. Everyone was lead to believe that we were going to have a graduation ceremony but it never happened. At this time I was the most desirable in my class so whatever girl I went after I got. My sons mother was pregnant and I wasn't anywhere to be found because my brother from another mother, Mr. prime, was constantly in my head telling me stories about them two having unprotected sex and how he ejaculated in her every time. He told me she was fucked up in the head and his reasoning behind this was that she tricked him many times telling him she was pregnant by him. He warned me not believe that bullshit so when I would run into a family member of hers my excuse "I'm just like the white man. You just can't tell the white man you're a high school graduate. You have to show him proof. So until I get proof my hands are tied." Her aunt agreed with my logic and I kept my word to the fullest that after the dna results proved little Dior was mine, I would visit him every day and spend time with my little man.

turns out he was mine and I stepped up to the plate. I would mash up bananas and feed him and sing melodies to him as a aby. When my lease was up it was a no brainer, I had to find room in a house to rent so I went back to the house on Iagnolia street. That turned out to be at huge mistake. While ving on magnolia street with three low life bums, none of my ommates were motivated to make money. The main hustler 1 that family was their father and he reached out to them and ntered them into his scraping hustle. I started working at /.I.S Western Inventory Systems where I was assigned to a eam that went out to stores like PetSmart and Victoria's ecret and counted all of their merchandise then gave them 1e total of each product they had in stock. While working 1ere I was permanently assigned to a team with this pretty ttle chick from Girard. I hooked up with her for a few reasons, 1ainly because she looked good, blew tree ,and was cool. The lacker the berry the sweeter the juice. She was so juicy I alled her slip and slide. We worked the same nights most of 1e time which was perfect for me

The house on Magnolia street didn't have any hot water or a working stove and a washer or dryer. To make matters worse one of the dickheads let some other dickhead bring in two flea bitten kittens into the house. Their reasoning for keeping the flea infected kittens was to take care of the mice. Thankfully every night me and the sexy girl worked together, I was able to sleep in a comfortable bed without fleas and take a hot shower in the morning. I would return uptown around noon and I started to notice that each time I returned to the bathroom sink and toilet it was black as tar. I'd be disgusted because I wasn't going to clean up behind three grown ass men. After a few straight weeks of me returning to a tar bathroom I snapped and demanded to know why they had to live so trifling. In reply the youngest replied, "We gettin money thats why." Moe Moe, the oldest, cursed the youngest out for running his mouth. He yessled, "Fuck you gone tell him our business for?!" Being the dude I am, I said "Hold up big guy. Don't knock the hustle. There's no such thing as too much money. Put me down." Then the oldest pulled me out on the porch to talk in private.

he conversation started out with him saying look my nigga
ve getting money off this junk. I raised my eyebrow and said
unk?" He said "Yeah nigga old car batteries aluminum cast
on anything we can get our hands on." I asked "Alright when
m I up for a payday?" He said "Slow down. We have to school
ou to the game." First I thought he was trying to fade me so I
aid "I catch on quick start schooling champ." I called him
hat because he was aspiring to get into the boxing scene. Ever
ince I was seven I would chill at their home and watch the
ldest and the middle brother spar. The only thing that held
im back was the problem that fucked up all our goals, drugs,
veed, wet and pills. After my drug abuse got out of control and
really started acting wild, the people I was dealing with on a
egular basis gave me an intervention. Havoc and my uncle
irk had a man to man talk with me about how the wet was
urning me into a zombie. They made my uncle D sit in on the
ntervention and both of us promised to quit. I held up my end
vhen it came to wet but the pills were a huge gorilla on my
ack.

I continued popping my blues and climbing trees while jumping through people's windows and hitting houses. I had my man Hell Rell driving me from crib to crib and coming up on flat screens and game stations. then we linked up with these whores from North Philly and me and the two girls each bought five blues but not Hell Rell. He stuck to the basics, weed and liquor. I was an amateur lockpicker so when he asked me to pop the lock on the liquor cabinet it was easy. My dumb ass took two double shots of cognac after popping five blues and now I was in my thief bag. The next move I made played a major factor behind me getting shot twice in my crown.

CHAPTER 10

The Game Changer

asked to use the bathroom then dipped off into the parents room. While inside I saw a safe and a gun box that contained a fresh 9mm HK. I put that in my cargo pocket then his little brother appeared and asked me why I was in their parents room. I acted higher than I was and said "Taking a piss." He said "The guests use the bathroom in the hallway. Look you way too high just go back downstairs with my brother." When got downstairs both girls were passed out on each other. Hell ell said they passed out before he could get one of them alone. e asked me to help him get them in the car we did the heavy et one first I ran in her pockets and came up a twenty in ddition to the HK back to Magnolia street I was the only one with a valid driver's license so I was in charge of driving I sked him from the get go were we trafficking narcotics ecause I can't get caught up I got my baby boy to take care of e was like naw we jumping over this wall and putting as many ar batteries and alloy car rims on the trailer as we can I asked him what were the rates he informed me that we get twenty five per battery and ten for each rim I went straight into Mexican mode loading two batteries at a time as well as two rims at a time after we loaded enough for a good score we rolled out we pulled over at a mile marker and dumped the scrap then we drove to the yard where they crush the cars twenty feet into the yard his father noticed a cast iron sink that weighed at least three hundred pounds so we deeboed it on the trailer then drove over to the claw the claw took each car he had on his trailer we rolled out he left his son with all the batteries and had me drop off the rims uptown so I did I asked the youngest to watch the rims for me so I rushed through the traffic to collect bull and the batteries so I scooped him and the batteries up dropped them off at the Dominican spot where they removed the tires from the rims after I dropped him off I went back uptown and got the rims we tipped them twenty dollars for taking the tires off the rims then drove to the scrap c drop off first I unloaded the batteries then the rims when we lifted the heavy ass cast iron sink it wasn't in the middle of the scale I told him to put it all the way on because whatever part f the sink isn't on the scale won't get weighed and we won't

et our full profit the manager tried to tell us it didn't matter

ut I had been weighing drugs on scales for four years I knew

ow the scale worked so we profited about five hundred and

ixty bucks he put the sixty aside for his pop and we split the

ve hundred so we went to pick up his pop he was really

issed off at his son his exact words were "I'm sick of getting

ɔbbed by my own sons

hen champ hollered back at him me and moe moe loaded all

ıe shit all your old ass did was talk and point I felt bad a little

it and gave his dad a fifty and told him I didn't feel right

eeping all the money if you feel like you were ripped off after

etting me paid he let us borrow the jeep so I took bull to my

art of uptown we got an 8th of purple haze from cufflinks and

rabbed a bottle of henny back topside I had Hell Rell's dad'

mm German HK I knew he would be looking for it soon then

remembered the whores were from North Philly around the

ıme area as my homie vest I thought that if any cop catches

ɔmeone with this strap it mines well be in North where the

itches were from and not Germantown where I I rested my

head so I hit vest up and told him I want to trade a strap for a strap but I'm going to need a strap and a hundred dollars because the strap I had was a 9mm heckler and Koch he said ok what kind of pistol you want I told him an old school special that's a .38 caliber revolver he told me he had two young bulls that had what I wanted and that they really need the HK because Norris was at war with Berks street I caught the xh and the 33 to 22nd and Diamond to make the trade I put on my pharmacy tech scrubs on to appear like an ordinary working citizen as the two bulls walked towards me an all-black Impala was shadowing them they looked scared so they power walked into the shop and rushed to make the deal the person in the "09 impala was a OG from berks so I told them to follow me upstairs I was scheming before I handed bull the HK I took the bullet out the chamber and removed the clip showing him the clip was fully loaded with black talons unarming them in case they wanted to get me after I did that I grabbed the .38 I was about to jam them for the .38 and the hundred dollars I gave vest that let me be me look he nodded me off declining my motion I knew he didn't need to be at war with Berks street

nd the young bulls so I played it cool and gave the young bull
he HK and took the hundred bucks vest said yo youngin
where my twenty for setting all this up young bull Said I have
o get you some other time vest I said NO that ain't right we all
rooked and we all know the middle man gets a connection fee
o I took a dub and blessed vest with it he asked me if I was
ure being a middle man myself I knew he was expecting that
ub I let everybody leave first when they got outside I saw vest
og to his car and flag the young bulls away I hit vest upon his
ell phone he answered and said "damn Reese where were you
when we walked out the shop Ol' head from Berks was
unning towards us with a .40 in his hand I was like I just
raded with young bull I told yall the ammunition are black
alons armor piercing bullets he should've clapped at old head
e said they only young bulls that's why I flagged them off I
wasn't gone get my wheel shot up I didn't get back topside
ntil sunset when I got to the door I noticed the glass on the
anel next to the door was broke it was wide open when I got
nside I see the neighborhood flea not that he was a bum he
ist had all the features of a flea braids that looked like

antennas and he was small I didn't trust him because he shot the youngest brother in the arm over a phone and he made a comment saying that he doesn't just shoot niggas he kills them so I hooked up the oldest brother with an Xbox360 I came up on he asked me what I wanted for it he didn't have no money so I thought of something better than a few twenties I said I'll trade u the game station for one of your scrap metal days he agreed and hooked up the Xbox I threw in madden and told the flea to pick up the sticks so I could bust his ass remembering his underling buck city felt offended because he's a Gangster Disciple and I pulled out my I l pod touch and threw on Gucci Mane' blood in blood out song and he walked off in silence I asked the oldest brother fuck was up with buck city he was like Momo you throwing up all these blood signs and dude a GD folk In my defense I said yall know I always throw on my nigga Gucci Mane and rock out so I'm busting the fleas ass with the Washington Redskins 14 to zero I had a funny feeling about the opening in the wall next to the door so I grabbed the door that had been broken for some time off the floor to cover the opening the middle brother called me over nd asked me why did I do that I told him I don't trust this flea

ooking mafucka or his GD homie from New Orleans what you

xpect me to sit here playing video games while he get his

unky to give me a head shot through the gap in the panel no

et I blew the flea out in that game of Madden as he leaves he

vas like momo freaky told me u traded dat hot ass heckler for

blue .38 he said if you ask me I think that was a Dumb ass

ade I replied I had my reasons bull for a male he talked a lot

lways giving people his opinion when they didn't ask for it so

e says what is a Blood doing with a Blue gun sell it to me

1omo you know me and buck city GD folks I was like oh really

nd decided to G-check him my homie little rock was from

etroit he was a Real Gangster Disciple every time somebody

aid he was lying he would stand in the six a GD stance and say

put that on the boss and put his forks up so I said to the flea

k so all of a sudden after buck city moved here to escape

atrina now u GD too huh he said hell yeah And put his forks

p I didn't respect or trust bull so I stood up straight looked

im dead in his eyes and and said if you are what you say you

re stand in the six confused he said fuck all that sell me that revolver you know I will need it a strap that keeps the shell casing after I blam a nigga I need that so I told him what I told every other person that asked to buy one of my pistols which was I don't sell guns this a small world see say I do sell you this piece and later on you find yourself in a jam and decide to sell it yourself what's going to happen if the person you sell it to tries me and I get shot with the same gun I owned he smacked his lips like a bitch and left freaky was like momo watch out that's the same shit that happened when my brother didn't give him the cell phone they robbed bull for I pulled out a Dutch and a bag of Kush and said a bar Gucci Mane said .44 snub nose hit you real close smoke the bubble Kush blood give a fuck folk the next day my homie D from chew avenue mom called me and asked me to ride with her to visit D because she couldn't handle seeing him like that alone waiting for them to call us some dummy left the key to his locker in the key hole now you know me MR. come up I stole bull bag took it outside and put it underneath D mom's car then set a reminder in my phone to go off an hour later reminding me about the bag I needed the reminder because D's mom was real had severely njured her foot and was getting the pills I liked for the pain so asked for three first she said no moe so like most drug addicts said please my lower back is killing me vulnerable knowing ow she felt when in pain she passed off to relieve my so-alled pain after the visit I grabbed the bag D mom shook her ead and asked me why did I steal that guys bag I said he umb enough to leave his key in the slot I'm smart enough to ake his stuff it was an old ass game cube pissed I thought to nyself who likes video games that they wouldn't care that ame cube is five years out dated I said to myself Vietnam H-an see he had all the hot ammunition so I traded the game ube for thirty dollars and four .38 caliber armor piercing ullets so illegal you'll receive five to ten years per bullet nat's why I only wanted four and not six to load the .38 I oaded it 2regular rounds   2armor piercing 2regular rounds nd so on and so on a strategy that ultimately saved my life

: was ironic that I was repping the G-shine Blood set and wned a blue armada Rosa revolver when I first made the ade I couldn't shoot it to make sure it worked because I was n my uncles place of business so when I finally did shoot it I was thrilled with the results mainly because I never knew revolvers could be double action pistols   we bombed the house to get rid of the fleas six times and each attempt failed to get rid of the fleas 100% so I started staying over my friend day brand's girlfriends' house not just at night like with the broad from Giraud I was kicking it over there basically 24/7 except mornings like I said every morning after the dna results proved little Dior was my son i hiked from topside all the way to Mount Airy avenue to feed bond and sing to my son his uncle little Dior and I would sit on the sectional and watch the

NFL network trying to get his mind accustomed to football I would bond with my son until his mother got off of work even when she got off I didn't leave immediately I would hold my son close and put his ear to my heart I remember reading somewhere an infant gets close to his or her parents by getting to know the rhythm of their heartbeats my child's mother was cool towards me even though the entire time she was pregnant I denied being the child' father turns out I was wrong but I redeemed myself by going scraping with the brothers and taking my profits and buying him something from children's

lace after my fifth day in a row buying him shirt and bottoms
·om children's place tulpehoken street had a block party
Iorton street threw one also this was around September
ixteenth the fucking flea asked me twice that day to buy my
;8 I told him NO twice my mother knew how I was supporting
ıy child on the low income at W.I.S and sporadic scraping
ᵢhen I got chosen to go that Friday my mother called me to
ome pick up some money so I could buy me and my son some
neakers I woke up around eight am that Friday September
ighteenth I blew a L with tha broad I was messing with told
er I'd be back after I came from the sneaker store on fifth
treet after I smoked then got sucked off it was about ten am
: was already about eighty degrees outside so I got a ride from
ᵢpside to Stenton avenue it was way too hot to hike it then I
ᵢent to get the money from my mother as I approached her
he shook her head in disgust then grabbed my arm tight like
ice grips and pulled me into the supply room of the beauty
ılon where we'd have complete privacy she started grinding
ıe up telling me to get my shit together or I was going to be
ollecting my little paychecks and scrapping to get money for

120

a while I told her I'd straighten up she gave me that don't play look that sent chills then through my spine then handed me one hundred fifty dollars of her hard earned money

So I walk to Vernon road and wait for the 18 bus to take me to Fifth Street I took the ride and got off at fifth and Olney walked to the closest sneaker store called my son's mother to ask what his shoe size was he was a size five at four months I purchased him a pair of black Chuck Taylors and grabbed myself a red white and blue pair of adiddas afterward I walked to the clothing store on Duncannon grabbed a pair of cargos and a red white blue and black t-shirt that said illy on it then I walked to the wine and spirits on the strip bought a pint of Henny and called up Monday met him on Ruscomb blew an L with him then   I asked him if he had some blues so I grabbed five for eleven dollars it was entirely too hot to have pills floating around inside me Monday knew that everybody would've but I was addicted and all he cared about was making a few dollars the one person I bought drugs off of that actually cared about my well-being was gub if it was close to eighty degree's outside he wouldn't even sell me three blues e would say if it's over seventy five outside you really houldn't have any blues but he'd limit me to two I first igested one Xanax at the age of fourteen kick warned me that lues can be real addictive after my first one I was hooked so fter I had my son's sneakers and my stuff I go back to the 18 us stop and went back uptown I should've went straight to iy son's home to give him the things I purchased him but I /ent straight to /magnolia street blew a L and took a nap for /vo hours after I woke up I walked to papi's on T&M grabbed pack of Newport's and called up the broad I was with that iorning she asked me to come give her the business I was red I really didn't have the energy to bust her ass so I roceeded back to Magnolia as I walked I was on the same idewalk as this skinny light skin male I was known around iere not to be played with so I just knew this bull was going) excuse himself I guess I put myself on a pedal stool because e walks straight and bumps into me without saying anything iy head told me to let it go but my gangster said who the fuck ; bull so I shouted out watch where you going buck he turns round with his eyes cocked he said" what you say pussy I repeated myself and said" watch where the fuck you going buck he apparently wanted a dispute so he continued staring at me and then said oh no ol' head do I really have to flame you I'm high thinking he's talking about gunplay I wasn't for all the talking but I wanted him to be clear about his statement so I said what youngbull so he repeated himself and said" do I have to flame your old ass then he reached for his shit quick on the draw I grab my .38 gun bunt him then said gimme your wallet and phone before I clap your young dumbass he handed me everything then I pointed the 8 at his heart and said run down the motherfucking block he was out like a light my big ass sweating from the adrenaline so I go back home on the mag everybody is home i tell these niggas about the youngbull that just tested me the pint of liquor I purchased is replaced with a gallon the oldest brother challenges me to a drink off I accept after we knock back ten shots or more everybody starts to leave I'm really shit faced pills and alcohol mixed together in over a hundred degree weather was a really bad choice when people ask me why .

CHAPTER 11

Consequences

fell sleep on the couch just zoning out but the fleas kept biting t my ankles. I got irritated and woke up. Five minutes after I ot up and there was knocking at the door. I grabbed my 8 and checked the peep hole. It was the flea and the Island ude. My first thought was to lay back down and ignore the oor so I laid back down on the couch. Then I heard them nock again so I put my earphones on to drown out the noise. ut these dickheads continued to knock so I became impatient nd annoyed. I got back up and swung the door open and said, What's good? Damn! I was asleep. When you knock on omebodies door and they don't answer that isn't a sign to eep knocking assholes." The flea apologized and said " T told s she seen you at papi's grabbing a pack of ports." I raised my yebrow and said "So?" He replied, "We broke as shit Moe, can 'e please get some ports?" I reached in my pocket and pulled ut four cigarettes and passed two to each of them then I took ut one more for myself. As we were smoking our cigarettes, the flea asked me where's everybody at. I told him they had to make a move he says they told me you just caught some wreck and the law might be coming to the crib to book niggas I told him I didn't know what the fuck he was talking about the loud mouth island dude draws and says why you lying man I saw the whole thing thank you for putting that lil wannabe tough nigga in check he stay running his fucking mouth pretending to be tough always talking about guns he don't have. I continued to play dumb mainly because I had no idea what angle they were coming from the flea sits down on the couch not inside the house the couch on the porch he started getting bit by fleas he was like what the fuck momo how the fleas get on this couch too I wasn't with all the conversation so I just shrugged my shoulders the island dude was like moe I got a Dutch u got any trees to put in this L? I was like naw I'm toasty enough bull the flea gets off the couch and sits down on the chair closest to the porch wall I was on tilts so I took the seat next to him for the next ten minutes we're bussing it up exchanging stories about the freak broads we ran through in that neighborhood something must've happened around the orner because out of nowherethere's a fleet of police squad

ars speeding down tulpehoken because everybody ran their

mouth about the confrontation that occurred with me and the

oung man the flea decides to play against my weakness and

ays momo you hear those cops they're probably coming for

ou chief I replied fuck out of here ain't no cops looking for me

men he says ok then why are three bike cops riding up

magnolia as we speak I gave him the I don't give a fuck look

men he said look momo give me your strap until they roll out

looked him dead in his eyes and said fuck out of here I don't

rust nobody enough to let them hold my pistol then he

roceeds to mind fuck me which basically means he got into

my head and lead me to believe what he was saying was true

o he repeats himself saying momo you really willing to get

ooked for assault with a deadly weapon and possibly armed

obbery I said" if it comes down to that then I guess so then he

aid wow momo assault with a deadly weapon is a five to ten

ears minimum sentence not to mention armed robbery that's

nother three right there again I look him dead in his eyes and

ay " that's not shit I can do that time standing on my head G he laughs and says " ok MR. tough guy you can do that time no sweat but who is your son going to be calling dad while you're doing your time standing on your head I stopped and thought deeply I said to myself wow this flea looking mafucka is right what type of father would I be if I got locked up because of sheer ignorance so I reached in my back pocket and said I'm trusting you Dog don't cross me and handed him the blue .38 he walks off the porch and begins to go down the stairs I rush over to the top step and shout if the fucking cops coming why are you walking towards them he turns around with the gun in his hand and says this why bitch and fires off a shot the pistol was a double action type of revolver that means when you pull the trigger once two bullets fire as soon as I heard the gun fire I dipped to the left I should've dipped way left in the middle of my attempt to dip the bullets both graze my right eye ball I dropped on contact collapsing down all fourteen steps fortunately Magnolia street residents are all a part of the neighborhood watch someone called 911 and minutes later I was rushed to the hospital I wasn't completely unconscious I was in and out of it on the way to the hospital I was allucinating I could've swore I saw the Temple university ospital T but I was way out of it the emt's sedated me I woke p in the icu in a room full of surgeons the first voice I heard ras DR. mark J kotapka' he said if you can understand the rords I'm saying put your middle finger up so I raised my left rm and put my middle finger up everyone clapped their ands and cheered in excitement then two detectives entered ne room and asked me what happened I told them I didn't now which was the truth my memory of the situation didn't ome back to me until much later a lovely nurse approached ne and said what is your name I stated my entire name Maurice Victor Young she gasped and said Victor P's brother om Germantown I said I'm his son she said oh MY God my aughter is close friends with your uncle I'm going to call him or you then she said in the meantime would you like omething to drink I said yes a double shot of Henny mixed rith cranberry juice please she laughed and said Mr. Young we o not serve alcohol in the hospital and even if we did I rouldn't give you any I apologized and said that's the norphine talking not me. Then she told me her daughter wasn't answering the phone so she asked me if I remembered anybody that has his cell I said just because I was shot twice in my head doesn't mean I lost all my memory then I Gave her my uncle P's number they hooked me up to another morphine drip after half they bag was administered into my system I dozed off for an hour or two I was woke up by this heavy ass arm nudging me and the person was repeating my name In a low voice I was still a bit drowsy from the morphine then after the person said moe one last time I knew I recognized the voice it was my uncle P I was excited I turned towards him and asked what had happened to me he said you know the nut ass young bull that shot one of the brothers on magnolia street in the arm over a cell phone I said yeah the flea looking mafucka he was like yea I was like wow bull a cold bitch P was like yeah he can't hold his hands so he shoot niggas instead then he asked me why he try to kill you I couldn't recall exactly what happened on the porch so I told him about what I said to freaky the night I trashed him with the Washington Redskins how he tried to convince me that I should sell him my blue revolver because he was folk And I was blood P asked me what I said I

eenacted the situation how I tested his G-status by asking him
) stand in the six and he didn't know what I meant so I recited
 bar from the Gucci mane kick a door song .44 snub nose hit
ou real close smoke the bubble Kush blood give a fuck folk P
ras like moe how many times I gotta tell you that blood gang
hit ain't worth it where them niggas at now while you're
iying up here in the icu with two bullets inside your head
uh? I was like you right unc forget all that B.S gang banging
hit it before P left he asked for my mother's number so he
ould call her and let her know what happened she rushed up
) the hospital asked me what happened I told her what I
emembered she started to cry i asked her to calm down and
aid I'm alive mom it's nothing to cry about she relaxed then
rayed for me I dozed off when I woke up I asked my mom
ince I have two bullets inside my head do you think I'm going
) make it through this and said she didn't know but Jehovah
ras going to watch over me and make sure everything' alright
 waited until visiting hours were over to leave when they
rere over he rolled out when they left I was assigned a one on
ne nurse Mr. Marcus the next day he brought a phone into my

room I called my mother first told her I was feeling better then I called my ace cufflinks told him I was shot twice in my head he asked me who did it I told him he didn't know bull then he asked me was in police custody I told him no then he asked why did my son uncle tell him I was probably in police custody i told him I wasn't again then told that I'll get back at him later my head was constantly pounding so I'd push the nurse light in nurse Marcus was reassigned when the new nurse finally got to me I said I can't take the pain give me a tranquilizer that was strong enough for a silverback gorilla he told me that's not what I needed then he went and got me two 5mg Percocet I chewed them up and guzzled some ginger ale   the pain did not go away I was in severe pain I kept calling out Jehovah's name to allow his holy spirit to be with me and to please sooth the pain away about twenty minutes later I fell asleep I was out and pain free for about an hour I woke up to a police officer knocking on my door she read me my Miranda rights then handcuffed me to the bed I asked her why was I being arrested she told me she wasn't at liberty to tell me I was furious but I kept my cool knowing that getting ignorant would have only worsen things for me he only cuffed my left hand to the bed so I took my right slid it under my blanket grabbed the nurse bell and clicked it until nurse Marcus entered the room when he saw me cuffed to the bed he said officer you know this patient has a severe brain injury patient he can't even get from his wheelchair to his bed by himself the officer said rather he can walk or not it's protocol he's under arrest for a crime just do your job and I'll do mine Marcus asked me what was my mother's number so he could call her and let her know what was happening so I gave it to him when she arrived the hospital security wouldn't allow her up because I was in custody she immediately called my brother when he arrived he asked her why wasn't my mother allowed to come in my room she told him that he knows the protocol for hospital patients in custody I could tell by the look on his face he was starting to get agitated but he kept his cool he asked the female was she a mother she said yes so he asked her if her child had two not one bullets inside their head wouldn't she want to see your child regardless if they were in police custody or not she said of course so he asked once more could our mother come

132

inside she said yes but asked her to talk in private for a second first   so he stepped out the room with the officer and my mother entered gave me a hug asked if I was hungry or not I wasn't so she sat down when the officer and my brother were done talking he came back in and asked my mother if me and him could have privacy so we could talk so she stepped out he asked what happened I told him what I remembered leaving names out of the situation then he stopped me from talking and said Moe look me in my eyes and answer this question I said alright what's going on he said Moe did you shoot yourself I looked him dead in his eyes and said are you serious me with my ego you know I'd never shoot myself he said I also thought you'd never steal from me but you did right I looked away in shame then looked back in his eyes and said no way would I ever try and hurt myself let alone shoot myself in the head how would I be able to shoot myself twice in the head he said ok enough then left the room my mom came back in and asked me exactly what happened again I told her this flea looking mafucka shot me twice in my head since my brother cleared things up with the hospital security I was allowed to have isitors so my aunt Tasha came up to visit when my aunt got

lere she asked me what happened I told her what I

emembered then showed her how the entire right side of my

kull was out I scratched my head showing her how I could feel

ly brain she was grossed out and told me to stop by me doing

lat I must've poked at a nerve because my head started

ching I had a splitting ache I pushed my nurse button to ask

or pain meds but it was too soon I tried to relax and breathe

l and out but the pain was so severe I turned to my aunt and

aid tash do me a favor she asked what I said pull the plug she

lughed and said boy stop being so dramatic you're not

ooked up to anything I see why she laughed a my mom

eturned to my room and told me she told security to put me

l the system as a dna patient that means do not announce

1st in case the flea bull wanted to come finish the job because

was in custody there were always two police officers in my

oom they couldn't leave until the bail commissioner read me

le charges and informed the amount of money my bail was

at at after two weeks in the custody of the PPD the bail

ommissioner arrived gave the officers copies of the police

report read me my charges ant told me my bail was set at a hundred thousand dollars when he finished he asked if there was anybody I could call to make the payment for me I told him they could keep me because no one was going to post ten thousand dollars for my bail after my arraignment I asked the police officer if I could read the report he told me NO because I might use it to work on a story to prove my case he was sitting in front of me with his chair angled towards my bed I read the reports as he went through them the one about the altercation I was being arrested for said I ran up on the boy hit him with a gun and robbed him I remained calm but got really upset when I read the one about my shooting it said I was drunk and high on the porch playing with my gun and I must've shot myself by mistake I was furious after reading that I had a feeling that one of dickheads I was living with was at the time was covering for the flea i so I used my strength to raise my head up far enough so I could see who signed the statement I couldn't make out the first name but all I needed was the last to confirm my suspicions and I was right the fact that one of the brothers threw me under the bus didn't surprise me   after I was released from the police departments custody the Philadelphia prison system took control of my custody the correctional officers noticed that I wasn't an flight risk so they allowed me to relax without shackles I continued going to the gym in Einstein for physical therapy after one session while returning to my room the cousin of the bull that shot me was walking down the hall he looked at me as if he had seen a host then I had a flash back of what my uncle P had told me which was dude was going around the neighborhood bragging bout how he had just killed me when the bullets entered into my brain they punctured the tissue that keeps my spinal fluid in my spine so csf cerebral spinal fluid began to leak inside my brain the neuro team said that it was too much fluid and that needed to be drained so they put a shunt in my back with a tube connected to my brain and my spine to drain the fluid the surgeon tried to rush the process by draining the fluid fast eventually the tube had gotten clogged and my blood pressure started to sky rocket I would sweat excessively and my head would inflate like a water balloon all signs of infection but nobody picked up on it regardless of showing signs of infection

I was transferred to moss rehab Elkins park this was late October every time I went down for therapy I began to go into shock head swelling body sweating blood pressure was far from normal I developed hypertension after three weeks of having hypertension my body went into shock I fell into a coma while in the coma I was transferred to state road and put in the infirmary inside the detention center   I went from two hundred and fifty pounds to eighty five pounds I came out of the coma in the middle of December my vocal cords were so weak from not using them I couldn't speak so the staff members would put their hands under my palms And ask me to squeeze if I understood what they were saying and I would but I couldn't move anything on my left side I was scared because I thought my entire left side had shut down but my fear went away when I realized I couldn't move my left side because I had lost so much strength not because I was paralyzed I would try to yell out for nurse assistance once in a while the words were on the tip of my tongue but I couldn't formulate the words my cell was right next to the entertainment area I heard the television every day I would et very aggravated because I couldn't speak two months out f the coma one day there was about six nurses inside my cell closed my eyes and said to myself that I was going to dig deep nd use all of my strength to ask if I could watch some elevision so I used all my might to get the words out of my mouth I was surprised because I hadn't heard my voice for a ong time it still wasn't quite my natural tone I was speaking eal low and my voice was crackly the nurses kept asking me o repeat myself so I said can I have a TV in my cell as clear as could one of the nurse said you can get you a radio but I don't now about a TV she said would you like that I shook my head es she said now I heard you talk so no more shaking your ead or squeezing fingers you have to talk to get what you rant so I took a deep breath and said yes the next day she rought me a radio and my mail it was two letters from my ttorney saying that the person that was pressing charges gainst me hadn't shown up to any of the court appearances it lso said that if he didn't show up the next four times the harges would be dismissed and I'd be released I asked one of ne nurses to set me up with a contact list so I could call my mother and tell her the good news the entire time I was incarcerated as a brain patient my mother was calling the hospital to find out when they were going to replace my skull she was relentless in her efforts to get my skull replaced and me out of prison her efforts didn't stop with her contacting the people in charge at the hospital she would schedule meeting with the warden and Lieutenant Robinson trying to find ways to get me released when nurse K returned to my cell with the list she told me I could put five people on it you know I put my mother first my aunt Tasha second third my son' mom fourth uncle P then my father last I never got around to calling him every day up state road was miserable for me see I'm a free spirit when I was home I was barely inside I couldn't stay in the house for longer than an hour so me being in an little cell in the infirmary unable to walk eat or drink was pure hell I couldn't eat because when I fell into that coma obviously I couldn't eat anything so a feeding tube was placed inside my stomach even after i came out of the coma and was able to speak the prison doctor that restricted me from eating and drinking her reason was that she didn't know rather or not the od I would've swallowed would travel directly to my igestive tract she was afraid that the contents might get aught inside my lungs and ultimately they'd get infected so he scheduled swallowing test for me which is a test where ou eat and drink different foods with a special ingredient nixed in it so the x-ray can follow where the food was ending p so for the first four months I was feed liquids through my tomach I never got full certain times of the day a worker rould assist another worker by rolling my bed into the ntertainment room with the television I'd be in that room rith about a dozen severely injured criminals most had hattered bones bullets stuck near major organs and two were aralyzed one of them was a cold dickhead because he was llowed to eat he'd sit right next to my bed in his wheelchair nacking on cookies a whole fucking bag with at least twenty ookies and every time I'd ask him for one he'd say sorry u an't because you might get sick one time he was in arms reach om my bed plotting I said yo D give me a cookie or I'm going) D-block the whole bag he laughed I reached quickly but ude was like speed racer in his chair he was out then I got loud and said to everyone in the room that niggas were going to start running their trays in or I was going to D-block their shit the one worker was like damn bull you thard as nails can't walk your left arm is out of commission and you still threatening niggas I guess I thought I was still that tough moe mobile or not so I started praying at least twenty times a day pleading with my heavenly father begging for forgiveness vowing that if he'd bless me with freedom and my bodily functions back that I'd never rob steal or get high again I finally saw the error in my ways I won't lie to you when I first came out of my coma I wanted bull head on a silver platter but after I prayed numerous times my heart was softened I finally realized that dude didn't set me back he actually gave me a new lease on life Jehovah God blessed me with a second chance to prove I was worthy of life and to stand up and become a man and take care of my son   I was highly depressed mainly because I was stuck in an hospital bed with a huge bedsore due to the lack of care while I was comatose they failed to rotate my body and stretch my legs out due to the lack of care my left leg became contracted which later on became a huge speed ump in my gait which is Latin for walking my first three swallowing test appointments were cancelled due to severe weather finally by my fourth month on state road the transportation company for the prison took me to my appointment for my swallowing test I was nervous mainly because a nurse had left a pitcher of water on my shelf in my cell in arms reach stubborn I grabbed it positioned it to my mouth then nurse L entered and said yo when they start letting you drink I said today attempted to take a sip the liquid was so thin I began to choke he was like I knew you were bullshitting I snapped and said" then why you let me try asshole he replied" I wanted you to see why you're not allowed to drink or eat so getting back to the actual test to determine wather or not it was safe for me to go from a liquid diet to a regular house diet first the DR. had me drink orange juice they set up the TV to display the test I could really see the liquid and food travel from mouth to my stomach you could see all the details from my throat expanding allowing the contents to pass through so I passed the swallowing test and the doctor that conducted the test recommended I be put on a house diet with thickened fluids so i wouldn't choke my first meal after four months of strictly liquid feedings was two trays of mac and cheese and a salami sandwich the fifth and sixth month I was constantly visited by my public defender Ms. Ingram she asked me questions about my mental and physical condition she got the judge to agree to release me on bail pending on my skull being replaced when Ms. Ingram informed my mother that when Einstein was ready to put my skull on they'd release me on bail that' when my loving mother really got on their case about my craniotomy she'd call everyday to get them to push my surgery date pushed to the top of their list when calling didn't seem to be working fast enough she'd catch the bus and demand to know why six months had gone by without anyone scheduling my surgery a week before my operation I was sent to Einstein for a CT scan afterward my mother continued to call and see in person Dr. K's neuro team she was highly upset when they informed her that they could not find my skull I was extremely upset and asked Michelle Christmas from the infirmary' schedule handler to request them to make me an prosthetic plate for me nly problem was that they didn't have a mold of my head so ney weren't able to even try DR. winters the prison doctor new just by looking at the inflammation on my brain that in rder to fit my skull on properly they needed to drain most of ne fluid but regardless DR. K proceeded with the procedure nyway three days before my scheduled surgery the bail judge nxed over the paper work i needed to sign to be released into instein's custody I was super excited after seven long months f nasty prison food and arguing over which television channel) watch I was being released prison rules were that when ou're being escorted to an appointment you're not allowed to nke anything with you I totally disregarded that rule the norning of my surgery I folded up the letter the bail judge nxed me stating that April 30th 2010 I was to be released from rison custody.

Chapter 12

Redemption

Once I was admitted in the hospital, the one correctional officer did not want to just return to the prison without getting confirmation of my release. She called her partner, but they couldn't get through which made me irritated so I reached into my sock, unfolded the paper and handed it to the C.O. She read it and called back to the prison rand was able to receive confirmation. She apologized for not believing me, uncuffed me and told me to stay out of trouble and left. Then the nurses hooked me up to an IV and wheeled me into the operating room. I asked about four nurses to call my mother and one elderly nurse offered to go and get her. She looked like she was pushing at least 85 years so as to not put any burden on her, I said "that's alright someone is calling her." But she insisted and asked my mom's name and walked out the room. A few minutes later my lovely mother walked through those doors and both of our faces lit up with big bright smiles DR. K's assistant approached us and asked me if I was ready I told him was. Then I said pray for me mom I'll see you when it's over

ıe anesthesiologist had me sign a waiver stating that I hadn't

ad any bad reactions to anesthesia in the past I sign and they

ut the mask over my mouth and nose told me to take ten deep

reathes and start to count backwards from one hundred by

ıe time I got to fifty I was out like a light when I woke up I had

 tube connected to the back of my head and the vital sign

ables hooked up all over chest my head was in extreme pain

ain so bad I began to cry so they attached my I.V to a deladen

rip a intervenes pain medication after the first bag I was

·ansferred to the intensive care unit where I would have to

tay for twenty four hours for observation to make sure

verything was draining correctly I called my son's mother

sked her to bring me two bug Buford burgers from checkers

was out of prison and ready to start eating like a free man

lus my legs were skinny like pencils and I was only ninety

ve pounds when I was used to being between two thirty and

ʌo fifty my aunt grabbed me a new cell with a different

umber so I could contact my mother and whoever I needed

ɔ reach because I made an oath to Jehovah God that when he

delivered me out of that situation that I was going to live life correct and do what he required from me from then on my main points were no more stealing robbing or getting high off of any narcotic ever I swore myself to a sober more simple life where I could focus on my son and be the best father I could be towards my son I asked my mother to set me up with an bible study with one of the elders from our congregation like I stated before I tried being a

Jehovah 's Witness before in the past but Satan had a firm grip on me unfortunately each bible study I had with an elder eventually got discontinued when my mother went to find an elder to become my bible study advocate most were unsure about my level of commitment this time around so my mother reassured brother Campbell that I was in it for real this time and that that close encounter with death woke me up and opened my eyes to see the error in my ways so he agreed to study with me he started by coming up to Einstein hospital we started out with the what the bible teaches publication because of the downgrading economy Einstein was forced to discontinue their inpatient therapy program but I didn't give p hope I asked my mother and grandmother to pray and ask ehovah to please open a door so that I may begin my ransformation back to the moe with the old physical apabilities not the old lowlife methods about one four weeks iter I was visited by DR. Sooja Cho she was surprised that I emembered her from "2009 when we first met she asked me I wanted to come to the Elkins park location of moss rehab I old her most definitely the next day while my mother was iere she explained to us how this was going to work out this me she brought us a handful of paperwork that needed to be lled out and signed asking me my needed medications and iet plan the day I was transported to Moss rehab Elkins park saw almost everyone that was there when I was in "2009 I emembered all their names they couldn't believe it after three veeks they removed my stiches and the bandages from my ead my cut was chopped whoever prepped my hair for the urgery must've had a sense of humor I say that because he cut very strand of hair but he left a medium sized patch on the ift side and in the back of my head because my lefts hamstring vas contracted I asked my physical therapist if a tendon release surgery was needed she informed me that we would use that as an last resort because the surgery wasn't a quick fix afterward there will still be a lot of stretching needed she also explained that the surgery might do me worse than it would benefit me mostly because the process of the surgery is the DR. basically cutting the muscle which would take very long time to heal and would weaken me which would be very bad long term for my gait so we began stretching I'd lay on my stomach for an half hour stretching my hamstring and hips it was pure torture for me for the first two weeks after my therapist noticed we weren't making much progress no more than one or two degrees at a time my range of motion was an negative forty five I needed at least an negative twenty two to be able to walk independently so she told me to stretch my leg as long and far as I could she had another therapist hold my leg in place while she put my leg into an cereal cast which would give me a twenty four hour stretch after three days with the cast on I couldn't bare the pain anymore my leg constantly would spasm up inside the cast that Monday she removed it those three days really helped me gain some range of motion I

ent from an negative forty five to an negative thirty five I
ained ten degrees in three days and we started walking with
post walker that's a walker with a sling for your arm I'd be
ble to do twenty five feet then my leg would cramp up my
herapist sat down and had an heart to heart conversation
ith me she told me that she was going to do everything she
ould to help me get back on my feet literally but I had to work
ith her and endure most of the pain because it would benefit
he in the long run so she put another cereal cast on my leg but
his time the prescribed a medication to reduce the spasms she
ecided to leave the cast on my leg for a week to give it that
onstant stretch trying to give me that range of motion I
eeded to be able to walk sleeping with the cast was very
ncomfortable my nights sleeping at moss were very limited
ven without the cast I'd constantly have nightmares
eenacting the trauma I went through I'd wake up sweating
nd paranoid I hardly got over six hours of sleep each night
hen I was used to eight or nine which in turn made me very
ritable during the day I was very short with the nurses and
ther staff often demanding things instead of politely asking

which I was raised to do but on the contrary the nights I did get my proper sleep I was the perfect gentleman no one had any complaints about me besides the fact I was very dependent I couldn't wipe my own rear after bawl movements nor could I cut my meals without making a mess getting dressed was very difficult until nurse cyd demonstrated how I could get my boxers and bottoms on easily she was one of the only nurses that was patient with me the entire time I was there after my therapist removed the second cast my leg went from negative thirty five to negative twenty five so the cereal cast method was working effectively but there was more work to be done in order to get my leg straight enough for me to start walking then DR. Cho told me about the Gait lab like I informed you before that Gait is Latin for to walk I asked her what did they do inside the laboratory she explained that for the paralyzed patients they hook them up to the rewalk machine I wasn't paralyzed so I didn't ask more about that machine I went on to ask if they do the tendon release surgery in that laboratory she told me that the tendon release surgery wouldn't benefit me she gave me the same reasons m therapist

ave me so I asked just what can they do for me she told me
1at they administer a series of shots into the hamstring
1jecting medication that would reduce the tone in my leg and
1at after I received the shots they'd put another cast on me
ne last time and I should have enough range in motion to be
ble to walk I was excited that I was in a facility that was doing
verything they could to get me back physically it was the
1iddle of May when my name was put on the list for the Gait
1b while waiting I continued to go to my physical therapy
essions stretching and laying on my stomach I was very
nxious I asked my therapist everyday where were they at on
1e list and was there any way that I could get bumped up to
1e next three patients to go she explained to me that they put
1e outpatients on as an priority because they have to travel to
et to their appointment and that whenever they were ready
or me all they had to do was send an escort to my room to
ring me down to the lab. Days went by I continued my
1erapy and stretching on June tenth a nurse was sent to my
oom to wheel my bed down to the Gait laboratory I was
xcited and ready for progress when I arrived I was

introduced to DR V. and her team they stretched my legs out and patted on my left hamstring I guess to make the muscle pulsate so they could inject the medication DR. V asked me was I afraid of needles I laughed and replied do you see all of these tattoos she said oh sorry for asking such a silly question i said no need for apologies you're just doing your job she prepped the syringes while one of her assistants sprayed my hamstring with an freezing agent I asked why was that needed her response was the process can be far worse than getting a tattoo so it's used to dull the pain she injected my leg about eight times afterward the same nurse wheeled my bed back to my room. I was extremely tired from the injections so I watched television and went to sleep the next morning was an typical morning at moss shower medication breakfast then physical therapy when I arrived at my therapy session my therapist was thrilled she felt as though since the cereal cast had made plenty of progress in gaining my range in motion back she decided that because I was getting discharged in five days that that would be a good amount of time to prolong the stretch and maximize the effect on the injections done to my ft leg so she put one on and the DR. doubled my anti spasm edication so I could endure the pain for my last five days ere my mother and brother decided to give me another hance so when I'd be discharged I was going back to my home ith my family I was really happy and relieved because I didn't now when my brother and I were going to patch things up etween us I'd been feeling really disgusted with myself for hat I put my family through that was the main reason why I owed to my heavenly father Jehovah that I would stay drug ee as well as never robbing or stealing again those last five ays at moss rehab flew by quickly my last day they decided weigh me in I was up to195 pounds I was finally getting back my normal weight but the nurses advised me to take it easy ainly because it would be harder for me to get on my feet ith my weight being too over bearing the breakfast I had that orning must've been old because my stomach reacted badly wards the meal hours after my food digested I found myself the restroom doing two things at one time vomiting and oving my bawls I was in no mood for therapy then my erapist sub entered the restroom where I was exposed and started rushing me saying she was about to get off and she was the only one there able to take my cast off I was highly aggravated and started showing my ignorant side after the nurse cleaned me up and helped me change my clothes I was wheeled down the hall to remove my cast my stomach was really doing somersaults I wanted to lay down I was sweating and my blood pressure had sky rocketed after she got the cast off I laid down on the mat and she starts pressing against my leg trying to get a measurement totally disregarding the fact I was in extreme pain. They calculated that I went from negative twenty five degrees to negative twenty after I returned back to my room I called my mother to inform her that I was coming home I also asked her to bring me up a change of clothes because the clothes they provided for me to change in weren't mine I tried to tell the nurses that the clothes didn't belong to me inside that facility no one but nurse cyd and renita listened to me I'm guessing because I had two bullets in my head they figured I was delusional but that was quickly rectified after a nurse from new york was assigned to me I could hear that New Yorker ascent thick in her voice so I asked her was she from ie Bronx or Brooklyn she said why yes I have to tell the other urses that they don't know what they're talking about I said what do you mean she then informed me that they all told her was out of it mentally and physically the physical part was orrect but I was shocked they said I was mentally acoherent getting closer to my discharge hour DR. Watanabe ld me the things I had to take care like call my initial neuro urgeon and see what he advised he also prescribed me sleep iedication after I signed the required forms I sat waiting for bout two hours then two beautiful women entered my room sked was I Maurice young I said yes they told me they'd be iking me home I called my mom to tell her to look out for me ecause I was on my way and my phone was dying. I arrived t my home my mother was there greeting me with a Kool-Aid mile she wheeled me down to her job everyone was excited) see me after seven long months I asked my mom if I could wheel myself over to Rite aid to drop off my script she was real ervous so she said no then her eyes began to get watery and he said in a cracked voice that she wasn't trying to be verprotective she just didn't want anything else to happen to me I didn't argue I understood completely she continued her customers as the sun went down more of her clients entered and the ones that didn't expect to see me were excited and asked if they could hug me I said yes you may so she finished all her clients her last one gave us a ride while in front of the house I was far from walking I hadn't even began therapy yet so my brother wheeled me up the grass and into the house the first thing I said to him was that I loved him very much and that I was sorry for almost making him loose his job I didn't want to mention the gun incident that early because I figured that subject was still a sensitive topic which I was correct he said ok and goodnight. The next day my brother called me into the kitchen so I wheeled myself to the table he started the conversation off by asking me how did I sleep and how did it feel to be back in the house my stomach began to tighten because I knew where this conversation was leading then he said Maurice I'm willing to forgive you of you just tell me the whole truth about what you did with my gun I was nervous so I lied he became aggravated and dismissed me from his presence ashamed I wheeled myself back into the room and pened my bible before I read any scriptures I opened out with prayer asking my heavenly father Jehovah to soften my rothers heart so we can form the same bond we had when he rained me years earlier our mother woke up and noticed my rother was aggravated she asked why they came into my oom and discussed it he told our mom that I hadn't changed I vas still the same lying backstabbing Maurice then he looked t me and said why can't you admit what you did I held my ead down in shame and said humbly I can and I'm truly sorry or the drama I caused this family and I will die before I cross ie ones that truly love me again he said ok it's about time you nanned the fuck up now it's time to get you up out if that damn vheel chair he walked over to me said use your arm rest to tand up I did what he instructed I was standing tall I had ctually forgot how tall I was because with my left leg ontracted instead of standing tall at 6ft"3 I lost two inches nd was standing up at 6ft"1 my brother told me to put my arm round his shoulder and walk with him I walked about five eet and he put my chair behind me and said that's enough for oday but by July you'll be walking to the kitchen I replied yes but by the time I turn twenty I'll be walking without any assistance he said that's what the fuck I'm talking about I said I can't thank you enough for forgiving me because you don't normally let anyone get over on you I love you for that he told me he loved me too but he was really pissed at the fact I was really trying to hold on to that lie so he wiped the slate clean the between us and every morning he'd work with my walking I'd put my good arm around his shoulder and take small steps towards the kitchen we'd walk to our piano and back to my room twice then would call it a day after a week of my brother giving me physical therapy I received a call from the visiting nursing association a Ms. Craig she came to my house and put me down for the independence waiver which got me connected with liberty resources Ms. Craig told me that after I got approved I could choose anybody I want to be my nurse I was happy about that and she also set it up so therapist would come to my house and work on my walking and arm movement I had Jerry for physical therapy Rena for occupational I didn't do speech when Jerry would come over for my session he'd bring a hemi cane or side walker which is n four legged cane you hold to your side to assist with your

walking the first time he brought it for me to use I walked my

rst one hundred feet my brother observed how good I walked

with the hemi cane and asked Jerry where could we go to

urchase one for me to use on a regular basis he told my

rother that he wouldn't recommend I get one until I perfected

ow I used his my brother agreed that it made sense for me to

et 100% used to using one before we bought my own. for the

ext two months I continued my therapy with the VNA then I

ot my initial neuro surgeon to approve me for outpatient

herapy I decided to go back to moss but the waiting list for

lkins park was very long there I met a very eager physical

herapist name MS. Swords and a very patient occupational

herapist name MS. Walker the physical therapist would have

ie stretch for the first half hour trying to get me below a

egative ten degrees I'd lay on my stomach with an heating

ad on my hamstring to loosen me up when my left leg got to

n negative seven degrees MS. Swords ordered me an hemi

ane for home I'd walk with it to get things out of the kitchen

fter a month of practicing with it at home I grew confident

enough to try to walk without it one day my mother was in the kitchen getting something and I decided to surprise her by walking from my room to the kitchen with no assistance I won't sit here and tell you I did it effortlessly because it took a lot of strength and determination because my leg wasn't completely straight yet I walked with a deep limp when I finally made it to the kitchen I said mom look I'm walking she said good show your son because he'll be over this weekend I was happy I was finally getting a chance to see my son in a home environment instead of an hospital when he came over at first he was distant but my mother and brother told me that if I want to become close to my son that I had to talk to him constantly so I'd put him in my wheelchair and wheel him back and forward and occasional wheelie after ten minutes of play time I'd lay him on my bed and start talking to him I'd tell him " Dior I'm your father me and your mother brought you into this world when you were first born your uncle and I would watch football with you and I used to cradle you in my arms and sing to you I also held your ear to my heart so you could get used to the rhythm then I would sit him up take a seat next him and tell him to listen to my heart beat after he'd listen or a while he would crack a small smile and that would brighten my day because it made me feel like we had a better connection for the longest when I asked him who am I he would reply Elmo I'm guessing that because he heard my mother and my brother call me MOE he just related it to ELMO that sesame street character my mother and I would laugh every time he'd reply you're ELMO he continued calling me ELMO for the next two months then one day I was in the kitchen eating and I heard my son rushing down the stairs screaming DAD DADDY DAD I was filled with extreme joy I rushed over to him and picked him up I said to him you finally got it huh then he shook his head up and down I smiled so hard then I went to my mother and thanked her for allowing my son to come over every weekend so we could get close on my birthday my mother took me to the Chinese buffet and we had good time and I thanked Jehovah for allowing me to see the age of twenty I continued my therapy at moss that Friday I had talk with MRS. Walker telling her my left arm felt extra stiff every morning and asked if she felt that the motor lab would benefit me so she decided to run some test on me to see how far I could extend my thumb and rotate my wrist she saw despite many efforts and exercises I was still very limited in my range of motion so she called up to Elkins park and scheduled me an appointment for January 14th MS. Swords figured we made all the progress we were going to make for the four months I had been seeing her I was now walking with an single legged cane and able to get up off the ground quickly in case I fell which she hadn't taught me my brother was the main person teaching me how to do things the year came to an end quickly my brother and I were growing closer he forgave me completely I could tell because he never brought up the incident again but once that time he did bring it back up I could see the extent to which I hurt him when I heard the pain in his voice and saw the hurt from betrayal in his eyes I swore to myself that I would always put family first and never touch another Narcotic again not even prescribed ones and I've been Narcotic free since September 18th 2009 I also swore to myself that I would never betray anyone in my family again. For the longest I couldn't look at myself in the mirror I felt so isgusted within I had become the family addict and thief it ras wasn't until my brother hugged me and kissed my prehead and told me that he loved me but he hates the choices made that I could bare looking at myself I thought I couldn't leep because of post-traumatic stress syndrome but now I ealize it was from the guilt after the year 2011 came in I asked iy brother to get me in shape like he did with me in the sixth rade he agreed but said we'll start out light and increase little y little everyday he'd drive me to this track he had me power ralk do squats and jump to strengthen my calf muscles after re did the pathway for about two weeks he advanced me to ie actual track we would power walk the first five laps on the ixth and last lap we'd jog the last one hundred yards I'd be weating very hard but never too out of breathe because when was younger I remember a young man that lived in the jungle old reporters that when he hunts he breathes in and out irough his nostrils not his mouth and that strengthened his ings an gave him more stamina and endurance so I did just iat after ever workout my brother told me to knock out one undred sit-ups so I did then I would fall asleep for at least six hours I was getting prepared for my visit with the motor lab on the 14th I arrived there at nine am grabbed some breakfast then went in they hooked the muscles in my arm up to a computer to see how it functioned there were six muscles that really needed the injections so he just injected them all I barely felt the injections I was instructed to wait two weeks before I resumed occupational therapy so I waited until the 21st to return when I returned on the 22nd I was introduced to my new physical therapist Ben MS Swords had left the facility I told MRS. Walker that I didn't want to be 21 not able to tie my own sneakers so she said ok let me teach you she instructed me to show her how I would do it first then she taught me two other methods and I had it well not 100% I needed more practice after two months of practice I was able to do it 100% I was very proud of myself and once again thanked Jehovah for allowing my bodily functions to come back to me a few days after I returned to moss I noticed the fluid collection on my left side increasing I also would feel the entire left portion of my skull move when I would sit up so I took my hand placed it in that portion and checked it's sturdiness I noticed that my initial neuro surgeon hadn't connected my skull completely so went to him for a follow up to see what we could do because this was an major issue if I fell and hit my head it could crack open like an egg so I Made my appointment when I got in he told me when they sawed of the bone fragment the electric saw damaged most of the bone destroying its structure so I asked again what can we do to fix the problem he told me they had a material called mesh that was knitted fiberglass he told me he could mend the bone fragments together by using the mesh I told him I'd sleep on it when I returned home I thought about the possible outcomes the main issue was if my bone was already protruding how was adding material going to smooth it out even though I didn't mention that to him it was still a major issue to me my mother told me to stop being an am and just be grateful that I'm alive and functioning better than most when it came to gunshot wounds to the brain but I wasn't a settler anymore I was determined to get back to normal so I called my insurance company and requested a list of neuro surgeons that they covered I received the list two weeks after the request so I googled all the surgeons on that list this time I wanted the best hospital in Philadelphia so I only googled the surgeons that worked at university of Penn out of all the surgeons I looked up I was most satisfied with Peter Leroux so I called and requested an evaluation they needed a recent CT scan so I called my primary care provider and asked her to order one for me my insurance approved that same day and I went three days afterward and got the cd report then I called back down and scheduled my appointment for the evaluation it was on June 16th of 2011 when I was called back to the room the nurse practitioner told me I had water on my brain and that that could cause major brain damage so he told me to come in on the 22nd to get a shunt put in I was nervous because that was the same device that made me fall into a coma I explained that to him then he told me the only reason I caught an infection was because whomever was my surgeon tried to drain the fluid to fast and the tube had gotten clogged but they were going to drain the fluid slow and steady he also told me that they had technology other hospitals didn't have or were too cheap to use he told me that they would get an 3D CT scan of my head and send the scan to a laboratory hat would construct a prosthetic plate that would fit my head orrectly I was filled with joy. That following week I returned Pennsylvania hospital early six in the morning went into urgery after forty five minutes the gurney I was on was being heeled to radiology so I could get a CT scan to check and see there was any excess blood inside my head the scan was fine I was transferred to my room where my mother was waiting me my head was wrapped up dry blood was on my ars and neck my favorite show Burn notice was airing a new pisode the next day so I asked my mother to pay for two days f television for me while I relaxed I watched Law & Order I as still tired from the anesthesia so I dozed off for a while en my roommate started making a lot of noise so I turned y television back on watched television until nine and asked e nurse for my anti-seizure medication and sleep medication ecause they had just operated on my brain they didn't want give me anything that would Make me go to sleep so he just ave me some Seroquel and I called it a night the next day I atched burn notice all morning around eleven A.M I was rought down to get the 3D CT scan the scan was sufficient enough for the lab to get an accurate mold of my head an hour later I was discharged and my brother came to take me home when I got inside his vehicle he was like damn bro you walking around like you never had brain surgery how you feel I replied I feel great on our way back home he received a call then asked me if I wanted to meet his Captain I said sure so we rolled over to his district he cap was like nice to meet you your brother is always bragging about how strong you are and how much of a fighter you are I smiled said yes sir I'm staying strong for my son then we rolled out and went home. So I relaxed and worked on this novel after a month of my fluid being drained slow and steady the portion of my forehead that was protruding had evened out with the rest of my scalp ben the nurse practioner for Peter Leroux called me in for a routine checkup he noticed my fluid was drained enough for the plate to be put on properly my plate was ready so that following Monday I went to the hospital and had my prosthetic plate put on. After my surgery I felt like a brand new Maurice they sent me to the intensive care unit for overnight observation when I arrived in the room the nurse informed me that my mother ad just left and went to the icu lobby so I asked her to get my om for me my mother was happy I felt good she put my elongings inside my closet then stayed for bout twenty inutes right after she left a man entered my room I sat up nd said excuse you chief what do you want he said oh my wife vas waiting for me in here I was wondering if she was still ere I replied look I'm the only one here ALRIGHT then this lickster walks over to my closet and opens the door I got real efensive and said YO YOUR WIFE NOT IN THERE THAT'S MY TUFF I said it real tough and aggressive because I used to be iat con-artist smiling in your face and stealing from you at the ame time he says " oh damn sorry man then left I immediately alled my mother and told her how some man tried to be slick nd steal my stuff I explained the situation just how I told you he informed me to keep my eyes open I also knew that after rain surgery they often suggest you get admitted into an ipatient rehabilitation facility I didn't want to so after I ate I ecided to prove I was far too well to get admitted into any ipatient rehab so after I ate I decided to clean up my mess I nhooked the vital sign equipment and started organizing my things how I wanted the nurses were like you must really feel good you're doing the janitors job and other stuff as the night went on I relaxed asked for my anti-seizure and my sleep medication after the medication kicked in went to sleep. The next day I met a nurse name Vince he decided he wanted to hear my story I'm pretty sure he heard it from his co-workers but he wanted to hear it from me so I explained to him how my gunshot brain injury was the result of me making a lot of bad decisions in my life when I showed him the picture I used for the cover of this book his jaw dropped and he just said you're a strong individual I told him it was only through the all mighty power of my heavenly father Jehovah that preserved me alive he was like you're really blessed then asked what I planned on doing from that point on I told him that I was going to keep a far distance from the lowlifes I was associating with get my book published and put all my time and dedication into being the best father for my son he shook my hand and told me he was going to get my discharge papers prepared for me so I called my mother and told her I was being discharged by noon she told me that she'll be there to get me as I waited I put the oom back to the way it was when I first arrived then this lovely nurse came to remove the bandage wrap from my head she warned me that it would be a little swollen for the first week but I could fix that by putting ice on the inflamed portion he also warned me not to lift anything that would make me strain she instructed me to give my scalp some time to mend then told me to call the neurology office the next morning to schedule a appointment to get my staples removed as I started to leave I asked her was it alright for me to put my fitted hat on she recommended it for outside in the sun but warned me not to have it on inside because the moisture would make a dark soft spot form I thanked the entire icu tem and told them to have a nice day then went to the lobby on the main floor to wait for my mother she arrived twenty minutes after I signed my discharge papers we drove to visit my grandma and aunt they were amazed that I was back on my feet in such short time I replied it's all Due to the power of Jehovah my grandmother agreed then we went home I remembered my surgeon told me that there was a slim chance that csf cerebral spinal fluid could leak through the plate until I healed all the way so I relaxed watched television thanked my heavenly father for giving me a second chance at life and I vowed not to screw up twice I told him that this time I was going to do things right then went to sleep for the night and I had the same nightmare that I had after I discontinued my studies for a short period of time the nightmare I had was a wakeup call I was on a baseball team Jesus Christ was the coach I was up to bat and you'll never believe who was pitching the dude that shot me twice in my head so I step up with my bat in hand got in my hitting stance dude put the baseball in his hand I was waiting for him to throw his pitch but my nightmare takes a turn and he pulls out the same blue .38 revolver shoots me in my head I fall the umpire shouts out strike one I get up ready to play ball get back in my hitting stance and he shoots me again in my head I fall the man yells strike two then I get back up coach Jesus walks over to me and says "son now you know the rules three strikes and you're out I wake up sweating grabbed my mother's clippers and took off my beard when I woke up in the morning I told my brother and my mom the wakeup call I just had and my mom took me to the mall I purchased three dress hirts and two dress slacks so I could return back to the ingdom hall after that nightmare slash wakeup call I decided ꜕ cut off all association with the dickheads I used to hang with nd decided to dedicate all my time in tending to my son. Now m on am journey to a better sober productive life so I can be man my son will be proud to call his father. 6.The things I've ꜕arned after everything I put my family and myself through I ꜕arned that you must always put your family first stay away ꜕om all drugs and any kind negativity I will always remember ꜕at bad association can alter your attributes and mold you ꜕to the type of people they are when I was nine ten and eleven told all my friends that smoked cigarettes and weed that they ꜕ere dummies and called them dickheads but besides the fact knew they were dickheads I still associated with them which fter all made me curious about the things they were doing I ꜕ill not sit here and blame the fact that I hung around people ꜕at did drugs in turn made me want to do drugs no that is not ꜕e fact in all reality I was curious and choose to smoke weed CP and popped pills but after I seen everything I put my ꜕mily through I will never return to that drug addict lifestyle

I'm at the point now that when niggas that I used to hang with call me I let it go to voicemail and don't even waste my time listening to the message I finally grew up and rose above all the foolishness so if you're traveling down the same road I was on and doing the same things I hope and pray that my life story opened your eyes to see that it's not cool nor will it get you where you need to be in life so I'm begging you for you and your families sake use my life as an example for what you shouldn't be doing recognize the error in your ways and change before it's too late.

Made in United States
North Haven, CT
31 August 2022

23501527R00096